MARTIN JOHNSTON

BEAUTIFUL OBJECTS

fi

The books from which this selection is drawn
were dedicated in the following way:

Shadowmass: for the poet's father

Ithaka: for the poet's sister, Shane

The Sea-Cucumber: for Nadia

The Typewriter Considered as a Bee-Trap: for Roseanne

Martin Johnston, Selected Poems & Prose, ed. John Tranter:
for Vivienne Bonney and Christopher Latham

Contents

Introduction — Nadia Wheatley	i
Acknowledgements	xiv

Selected Translations

Pass By My Country	2
To Be a Kleft	3
The Death of Dhiyenis	4
The Witch	6
Kitsos' Mother	7
Old Horoscopes	8
The Theft	10
Naxos	11
On Stage	12
Drinking 'Sans Rival' Ouzo	16
Elegy	17

Selected Poems

To Greece Under the Junta	20
In Memoriam Phan Thi Mao	21
Undergrowth	22
Sequestrum	24
To the Great Anger of the Nubians	25
Spinoza	29
Letter to Sylvia Plath	30
The Sea-Cucumber	32
Mazurka for Buzzing Fly	34

Gradus Ad Parnassum	36
Fault Line	39
The Blood Aquarium	40
Moriarty at Reichenbach	56
Critical Notes on Marcel Proust	58
Cave	59
Uncertain Sonnets	61
1. (airport)	61
2. (the decisions)	62
3. (vernal equinox)	63
4. (for George Seferis)	64
5. (directions for dreamfishing)	65
In Memoriam	66
Microclimatology	69
1. Pebble	69
2. The Unreality of Roosters	70
3. Winter Solstice	71
4. The Evidence	75
5. The Rent	76
6. The House	77
7. Notes from the Noctarium	78
8. The Benefactors: Mr. Achillopoulos' Mercantile School (Mt Pelion, Thessaly)	79
Cyclops Songs	83
1. Esprit De L'Escalier	83
2. The Afterimage	84
3. Goya's 'Colossus'	85
4. The Homecoming	86
5. Some Versions of Pastoral	87
6. The Recidivist	88

The Typewriter, Considered as a Bee-Trap,	89
Aristarchus and the Whale	90
Annula	92
To the Innate Island	94
1. The Shadow Screen	94
2. Finding Islands	96
3. The Ikonostasis	98
4. Cross In The Water	99
5. The Monemvasia Causeway	101
6. Friezes	102
7. From the Folk-Song Archives	104
8. The Bills	106
9. A Drink at the Exploding Monastery	108
10. Psychopannychy	109
11. Water-Garden Snapshots	111
12. The Whistlers of Phaistos	113
Windows	116
Reading Moby-Dick Backwards	117
The Secret War	118
Bonsai	119
Bolas	120
The Scattering Layer	121
The Brazen Head	122
In Transit: A Sonnet Square	124
1. Duende in Darlinghurst	124
2. Biography	125
3. Hecate County	126
4. The Rout of San Romano; or, Arsenal 3 Manchester United 2	127
5. The Modern Primitive	128

6. The Café of Situations	129
7. Games and Pastimes I: Chess	130
8. Games and Pastimes II: Crossword	131
9. Games and Pastimes III: Jigsaw	132
10. The Plato's Cave Hotel	133
11. Of Time and Typing	134
12. Drinking Sappho Brand Ouzo	135
13. For the Cretan Maker	136
14. On Aggression: Group Self-Portrait as Greylag Goslings	137
Room 23	138
For the Birds: The Life of Paolo Uccello	139
In the Refectory of the Ognissanti	140
His Wife is a Well-Known Criminologiste	143
Poise	144
The Battle of Trasimene	145
Hengist and Horsa	146
Sweet Dreams	147
Biennale, After Magritte	148
Biennale: The Romanian Pavilion	149
Gorey at the Biennale	150
Central American Football	151
Tabula Rasa	152
Getting to Know the General	153
Writing in the Manner of ...	157
Grief	158
Notes by Martin Johnston on 'To the Innate Island'	161
Copyright	168

Introduction

Nadia Wheatley

Martin Johnston *looked* like a poet.

The first time I saw him, he was sitting in the arched sandstone embrasure of one of the windows of the pseudo-Gothic building that housed the English Department at Sydney University. Dressed in a black skivvy and black pants so tight that they seemed to have been sprayed onto his pencil-thin frame, he was smoking a black Sobranie cigarette. Its clouds of aromatic smoke added to the halo-effect created by the sunlight catching on the split ends of his long, fine, dark hair. Yes, obviously a poet.

Whenever any of us other students in the Second Year Honours seminar voiced an opinion, our tutor immediately asked Martin Johnston what *he* thought. He seemed to know everything about everything. At the end of class, she always pounced on him, and interrogated him about his parents.

Yes, he was *that* Martin Johnston. Son of Charmian Clift, who had a weekly column in the *Sydney Morning Herald*. Son of George Johnston, whose novel *My Brother Jack* had won the 1965 Miles Franklin Award. In the latter half of the 1960s, it seemed that you could barely open a newspaper without reading about this gilded couple who had returned from a decade of expatriation in Greece to take the Australian literary world by storm.

Did Martin choose poetry as his genre because it was something his parents didn't write? Perhaps. Nevertheless, poetry was exactly the right vehicle for his particular mind and his particular voice. I don't intend here to attempt to assess his work, but if I can assist new readers to connect with his voice,

I will have done my job. Gentle, polite, and interspersed with laughter or with a phrase from some other poet—Dunbar, David Campbell, Seferis, McGonagall—Martin Johnston's distinctive spoken voice was an innate part of his written voice, and is the entry into his poems.

If there is such a thing as a poetry gene, Martin got it from his mother, who had won a poetry competition in her local area when she was nine years old. By the time Martin was born, in November 1947, Charmian had long since given up writing the stuff, but she used to recite it while pushing Martin and his sister Shane (fifteen months younger) in their pram. Although Martin imbibed the rhythms as well as the language of his mother's extensive repertoire at a time when other children were learning nursery rhymes, he was never a snob about poetry. While he would often break into one of the poems he had learned in this fashion, it was as likely to be Chesterton's 'Lepanto' as something by T. S. Eliot. Tennyson's 'Sir Galahad' was another that Martin had a habit of quoting. ('*My strength is as the strength of ten because my heart is pure.*')

In 1951 the family moved from Sydney to London, where George Johnston ran the European office of Associated Newspapers while Charmian did the day-shift on the couple's latest collaborative novel. Already reading and writing, Martin paid many visits to the Sir John Soane Museum (which would later work its way into a poem), and to the British Museum, where he had long conversations with the Curator. Delighted by his son's precocity, George called him 'the Professor', but Charmian was concerned that, restricted by the urban environment and the English weather, he didn't know how to play outdoors.

By the time Martin was ready for formal education, his parents had thrown in their swanky lifestyle and migrated to the remote and poverty-stricken Greek island of Kalymnos, where in the New Year of 1955 the two English-speaking children were enrolled in the local school. As Charmian Clift describes wonderfully in her first travel-memoir, *Mermaid Singing*, Martin discarded 'the beloved and familiar heroes of his imagination ... for a new crop of strangely-named *pallikaria*—Kolokotronis and Athanasios Thiakos and Miaoulis and Bouboulina'.

These brigands and pirates who led Greece to victory in the War of Independence were Martin's role models for the rest of his life. Yes, the Homeric alpha males were important, too—Ajax and Achilles and Agamemnon and all that crew— but it was the *pallikaria,* clad in their battle-stained white kilts and bedecked with pistols and daggers, who captured Martin's heart. And the ballads about them became a lifelong passion.

That year, when the island's primary school held its Speech Day to mark the arrival of the long summer holidays, Martin stood up before the assembled Kalymniots and recited one of these ballads in his brand new Greek tongue. I think this was just about the proudest public moment of his life.

When that summer was over, Charmian and George moved to the more civilised island of Hydra where, within a few months, they bought a house and had another child, who was given the heroic name of Jason. The Greek sojourn was now a long-term commitment. Apart from a miserable term at a Secondary Modern in England and a final year of high school in Australia, all of Martin Johnston's schooling took place in the Greek state system of education. The curriculum, with its focus on history and the arts, suited him down to the ground, as did the requirement to memorise slabs of poetry (notably that of Homer). Martin learned ancient Greek, he learned *katharevousa* Greek (the artificial hybrid conceived in the late 18th century), and he spoke and wrote *thimotiki* (demotic Greek).

Martin Johnston did not speak demotic Australian. But his Greek (even though it had a trace of an accent—unlike that of Shane and Jason), was the people's Greek. I realised this to my astonishment when we arrived in Athens in December 1975. At the airport, Martin jumped into the front seat of the taxi, and for the entire trip to our hotel he talked non-stop with the driver.

'What were you talking about?' I asked as soon as we reached our hotel room.

'Oh—politics ... music ... football ...'

Football? I looked at this new boyfriend with astonishment.

Over the following three years that we spent in Greece, this was Martin Johnston. Whereas, in Sydney, Martin's friends were fellow poets and critics and chess players, in Greece he could make friends with anyone. With the exception of Grace Edwards (Big Grace, in George Johnston's novel *Clean Straw for Nothing*), Martin avoided the foreign colony. We did not even go to the island of Hydra, except for a single miserable night at the very end of our three-year sojourn. When we lived in the town of Chania in north-west Crete, Martin's closest friends were Nikos Papasifakis, the middle-aged proprietor of our favourite *kafeneion*, and Katina Androulidaki, our bed-ridden octogenarian landlady. Together with Grace Edwards, they are the dedicatees of Martin's long poem 'To the Innate Island'.

But to return to the matter of where his poetry came from...

For Martin, as for all children, informal education at home was as important as anything learned at school. At the gatherings of *xeni* at the Johnstons' Hydra house there would often be poetry readings—either recitations from Charmian's well-thumbed copy of *The Oxford Book of English Verse*, or new poems written by one of the visitors—such as an unknown Canadian folksinger named Leonard Cohen, or the young Australian poet Rodney Hall.

One memorable day, a book arrived from Australia: the editorial team at Angus & Robertson had sent George and Charmian the company's new edition of *Australian Bush Ballads*. To ten-year-old Martin, it was a revelation to read these works that in some way resembled the Greek folk poetry he loved, but which were written in the unfamiliar Australian language. He went through the book, giving the poems marks out of ten.

Nothing received the full quota, but 'The Death of Ben Hall' got a top score of nine. It is easy to see the connection with *kleftika* ballads in this poem's allusion to 'the outlaw' who 'stole like a hunted fox through the scrub and stunted heath'.

Other books came by mail order. Lots of them. Cash was often short and sometimes non-existent, but Charmian and George had an account at a London bookshop. So Martin's reading in English was well covered.

But as to *writing* in English... I feel I need to stress that Martin Johnston's daily writing throughout his crucial formative years was done in Greek. Because of this, he brings a European, and particularly Greek, sensibility to his work. As he explains in his introduction to *Ithaka*, his selection of *Modern Greek Poetry in Translation*, 'The ambience of Greek poetry is different from that of poetry in English.' He adds, 'The Greek language lends itself very easily to flamboyance and the large gesture.' Quite. Martin's own work also at times lends itself to that—though mostly, when it does so, the voice is a touch sardonic. Martin frequently sent himself up, whether in his writing or in his conversation. And although poetry was his passion, he made no claims for it.

In an interview Martin did with his friend and fellow-poet, John Tranter, in 1980, he reflected on his practice. He was not interested, he said, in 'committed poetry, or poetry of explicit statement, or particularly in communication'. Rather, he was 'interested in making things, objects constructed out of words'. After remarking that Tranter had taken him to task for his 'obsession with chess: as you say, "a beautiful but useless game",' Martin went on to say, 'I tend to think of poetry, I must admit, substantially in terms of beautiful but useless objects.'

Hence the title of this selection of his work.

Martin was turning seventeen in late 1964 when he and his mother and two siblings arrived in Australia, where his father had come some months earlier. One of the main reasons for Charmian and George's decision to return from their decade-long exile was the desire to offer the children the chance of an Australian education.

Martin went straight into the final term of Fourth Year at North Sydney Boys High—an academically selective school where there were enough other oddballs for him easily to make friends. One of these was a boy of Greek parentage named Lex Marinos, who had grown up in the climate of prejudice common to the era. In his memoir, *Blood and Circuses,* Lex movingly describes how 'Martin was the first Anglo of my own age who made me feel good about being Greek.' He adds, 'Martin was a misfit in a variety of ways—he was bookish, non-athletic, eccentric, kind of foreign, and, above all, he didn't give a shit.' In class 'he spent his spare time translating T.S. Eliot into Greek, when he wasn't also writing his own poetry'.

By the age of eighteen, Martin knew what he wanted to do with his life. In a fragment of footage of a television interview conducted in the Johnston home in August 1965, he and Shane murmur to each other in Greek as their parents—seated in front of them on a couch—respond to the interviewer's questions. At one point, George remarks that 'Martin says he wants to be a writer.' Swivelling his head around towards his elder son, he checks: 'Do you still?'

'*Of course*!' There is something in Martin's tone, beyond the passive aggression of any teenager who is put on the spot in public. It is as if he is saying: 'What else could I possibly be?'

'We try to talk him out of it,' his father concludes. In fact, George, who had missed out on a tertiary education, desperately wanted Martin to have a career in academe.

At the end of that year, Martin did the Leaving Certificate and matriculated to Sydney University, where he immediately took to the rambunctious social life of pubs and parties, share-houses and psychedelia; from the music of Bob Dylan to the hippy-style clothing, the Sixties were made for him. Mature in comparison with most of his peers, Martin formed deep relationships with his girlfriends—relationships that would become lifelong friendships when the romance ended. Although he was never a joiner, his participation in the anti-war movement caused him to get arrested on two occasions. And, after the right-wing Junta seized power in Greece in 1967, he read poetry at rallies organised by the Committee for the Restoration of Democracy in Greece, of which his mother was one of the vice-presidents.

Amidst all of this, he was picking up university literary prizes for short stories as well as poetry. But the formal study of Literature was another matter. Perhaps things might have been different in another era, but the atmosphere in the Sydney University English Department was poisonous and highly politicised, as Leavisites battled anti-Leavisites for control of the curriculum. Martin could simply have stayed on at university, for the sake of the lifestyle. Instead, in mid 1968 he dropped out without completing his degree, and—to the horror of his ex-journalist father—took up a cadetship with the *Sydney Morning Herald*.

It is difficult to imagine a job less suited to Martin Johnston. Assigned to police rounds, he hated ringing up strangers and asking them questions in the aftermath of a personal tragedy. Nor was his ornate and scholarly prose style suited to the column he ghost-wrote for surfing legend Midget Farrelly, let alone to 'Dog of the Week'—a weekly column appealing for a home on behalf of a long-term detainee in the RSPCA pound, which Martin was obliged to visit in the company of the newspaper photographer. Aware that, if his plea failed, the poor creature would be given 'the Death Needle', soft-hearted Martin tried to make the strays more attractive by giving them interesting names. It was when he christened a particular pooch 'Cerberus' that the sub-editor reached breaking point. Back came the rebuke: 'No classical references in "Dog of the Week"!'

By now, it was clear that George Johnston's chronic lung problem, from which he had suffered for more than ten years, was not going to get any better. He had spent three long stints in hospital, but by late 1968 there was nothing more that could be done by medical staff, and he had been sent home to die. Charmian, who was carrying the burden of supporting the family emotionally and financially, was struggling to cope. Although both were drinking heavily, as they had done for years, the family GP would later insist that 'alcohol was not a significant health problem for either Charmian or George'. Their relationship was also, as always, combative, but (as Jason Johnston describes it) 'there was also an enormous element of camaraderie, support, mutual loyalty and love'. In June 1969, the couple celebrated their wedding anniversary by taking a holiday together on Norfolk Island. Barely two weeks after this, Charmian Clift made a suicidal cry for help, which turned into the real thing. A year later, in July 1970, George Johnston died in his sleep, at home.

'I was appalled at my mother's death, coming as it did and when it did,' Martin would say in an interview he gave for the National Library oral history collection in 1980. 'Whereas when my father died, it was tragic and terrible; it was also something that we had all very much been expecting, himself included, for a good many years.'

It was around the time of George's death that Martin gave up journalism in order to write full-time.

Already, he had put together a collection of thirty-three poems under the title *shadowmass,* which was to be published by Sydney University Arts Society. Delays in the production would mean that by the time this appeared, the poet had well and truly moved on.

Whether it was the additional time he now had for writing, or whether his grief over his parents' deaths meant that he finally had something significant to say, the elegies he wrote for his parents are in a different league from the work he'd previously been producing. While these two poems reflect the very different personalities of their subjects, they also encapsulate the dual nature of Martin Johnston's writing. 'Letter to Sylvia

Plath' is by the European Johnston: gestural and flamboyant, it follows a formal rhyme scheme. 'The Sea-Cucumber', with its conversational account of the time when 'we were all waiting', is written in a language as laconic as George Johnston's own broad Australian.

Somewhat to Martin's embarrassment, it was these two poems that brought him to the attention of the wider poetry world. After initially appearing in the September 1970 edition of the *Union Recorder*, 'Letter to Sylvia Plath' was published in the December edition of *Poetry Magazine* (soon to become *New Poetry*) and was chosen for that year's *Poet's Choice*. 'The Sea-Cucumber' had meanwhile appeared in the October edition of *Poetry Magazine*.

Over these same months, Martin was working on his first long poem, 'The Blood Aquarium', which appeared in *New Poetry* in April 1971. The voice is that of the mature Martin Johnston and the long form gave room for the breadth of knowledge that inevitably led to his work being called 'erudite'.

Of course, poetry wasn't going to pay the rent. But unlike most of his fellow-poets, who embarked on some sort of a career or at least took on a series of poorly paid jobs, Martin eked out a living as a freelance critic. By 1972, when he and I started living together, he was writing regular reviews for the Saturday book pages of the *Sydney Morning Herald*, for which he was usually given that week's would-be literary masterpiece. As the second-string film reviewer for the *Sun-Herald*, however, he was assigned to all the rubbish. I remember a particularly ghastly Friday when we watched *Blood, Sweat and Gunpowder*, followed by *The House that Dripped Blood*, and finally—with the aid of 3D spectacles—a Scandi porn flick called *Dagmar's Hot Pants*. To recover, we went to a newly opened restaurant called Tony's Bon Gout, where we splurged the whole of the review-fee.

In 1973, Martin published *Ithaka, Modern Greek Poetry in Translation*. Although he had been working on some of these translations since his school days on Hydra, he regarded the book's publication at this time as part of his public stand against the Junta. As he explained in the Introduction, by 'Modern' he meant poems written in *dhimotiki* Greek; he added that he had 'cheerfully ignored anything written in *katharevousa*, the artificial and archaizing "purist" language... recently reinstated as the sole teaching medium by the thugs and yokels who currently run the country'.

Along with many other Hellenophiles, Martin would not go to Greece while the Colonels were in power. In July 1974, the Junta fell. In November 1975, Australia suffered its own *coup d'état*. We exchanged Australia for Greece forthwith. In his luggage, Martin had the T-shirt with the Bruce Petty cartoon that he wears in the photograph on the back cover of this book. It shows an enraged Gough Whitlam wielding a ballot box like a sledgehammer. Alas! We arrived in Athens to the news that Malcolm Fraser had won the December election in a landslide. We did not return to Australia until the latter part of 1978.

Glimpses of that sojourn can be seen in a great deal of the work in this volume. As Martin would say in his National Library interview, 'After a long hiatus, in which I hadn't written all that much poetry ... suddenly things seemed to be going right again. It was going back to Greece that did it.' From 'Microclimatology' to the long poem, 'To the Innate Island', the poems spring from the places where Martin and I lived (Chania in Crete, Paralion Astros in the Peloponnese) and some of the places we visited. Mount Pelion, Yannina, Mystra, Monemvasia, Phaistos ... Martin's notes for 'To the Innate Island' provide a kind of diary of our pilgrimages.

Then we did something stupid. Missing bookshops and the company of other writers, we moved on to London, where we were too poor to buy books and could not work out how to meet English people. A few poems came out of that dreadful winter, but our partnership did not survive.

It was soon after Martin's return to Australia that he fell in love with Roseanne Bonney, whom he would later marry.

Martin had never wanted to have children, but he delighted in the company of Roseanne's daughter, Vivienne, who was fifteen in 1979 when he moved into their Darlinghurst household.

The next year, Martin joined the fledgling Special Broadcasting Service, where he would work, both as a Greek subtitler and as a sub-editor, until 1989. With its cosmopolitan staff and its commitment to multiculturalism, this was a place where Martin Johnston could be both European and Australian. But the job sapped his creative energy.

Beautiful Objects opens with ten works from *Ithaka, Modern Greek Poetry in Translation* (1973). As well as some anonymous folk ballads that Martin had been working on since he was a schoolboy, there are translations of the work of contemporary poets, including the Nobel laureate George Seferis and the left-wing activist Vassilis Vassilikos, then living in exile.

In the *Selected Poems*, the first six are taken from *shadowmass* (1971). Despite the writer's repudiation of 'committed poetry', I have included 'To Greece Under the Junta' and 'In Memoriam Phan Thi Mao', to give a sense of the poet's politics.

I have placed Martin's two elegies for his parents together at the opening of the works selected from *The Sea-Cucumber* (1978). The bulk of that book was written in Sydney from 1970 to 1975 but, as I explain above, the poems titled 'Microclimatology' were written in Greece over 1976 and 1977.

Moving on into *The Typewriter Considered as a Bee-Trap* (1984), the title poem was written in Paralion Astros in 1976 (I have a photograph of Martin typing on the cottage balcony on the day the poem describes), but he held it back to accompany other poems written in Greece, including the major work, 'To the Innate Island'. 'Bolas', 'Bonsai', and 'The Scattering Layer' were produced in London in 1978. 'In Transit: A Sonnet Square', begins and ends in Darlinghurst, but was mostly written while Martin was undertaking a solo trip to Athens and Hydra in 1979. 'Room 23' is also from that unhappy time.

A decade's silence follows that suite of work. It was in this period that Martin worked full-time for SBS.

Most of the final fifteen poems in this volume were produced in Tuscany, where Martin and Roseanne took an extended break in 1988. In a rare letter written to Vivienne that July, Martin was so confident about this return to work that he said, 'The way things are going, it looks as if I'll have a (totally unexpected) new collection of poetry ready for publication when we get back.'

That was not to be, but a dozen of these poems were published in *Scripsi* in February 1990, a few months before Martin's death. The same edition of the journal included a review of Umberto Eco's *Foucault's Pendulum,* written with all the brilliance and (dare I say) erudition typical of Martin Johnston.

After Martin's return to Australia in early 1989, his drinking took on a new dimension. The death of his half-sister, Gae, in tragic circumstances seemed part of a pattern with the deaths of his parents and of his sister Shane, who had taken her own life in 1974. Martin's grief was mingled with a kind of survivor guilt that caused him to talk as if his own premature death was also predestined.

In the way of such things, this proved to be a self-fulfilling prophecy.

His wife, his friends, his brother Jason, and I myself—we all undertook various projects to get Martin off the grog. He put up with us politely, patiently, but ultimately he went back to the pub.

Bloomsday (16 June) was always a milestone in Martin Johnston's year. Back in 1972, Martin had hosted a famous Bloomsday party at which the floor-to-ceiling brick-and-board bookshelves had collapsed onto the assembled guests. In 1990, he paid his respects to James Joyce's *Ulysses* by going on a binge with his drinking pals at the Toxteth Hotel in Glebe. After a few hours, he suffered a fit, and was taken by ambulance to Royal Prince Alfred Hospital. When triage staff began their assessment by asking him what day it was, he replied (politely as always) that it was 'Mr Bloom's Day'. The nurses thought he was rambling. He was diagnosed as suffering from *delirium tremens* and pneumonia.

Some forty-eight hours later, as Martin lay unmonitored in a hospital bed, he had a severe heart attack, which caused his heart to stop. When he was discovered, his heart was re-started, but he never regained consciousness. I arrived at the Intensive Care Unit on the afternoon of June 18 to find him living with the aid of a machine. With great generosity, Roseanne invited me to remain with her at Martin's bedside. I had taken his four books of poetry to the hospital with me, and I read them aloud to him, from cover to cover, over and over. As the nurse kindly said when I asked permission, 'It couldn't hurt.'

On the afternoon of June 20, the doctors came and turned off the machine. The striped curtains of the hospital cubicle were closed around us. Reminded of a mediaeval jousting tent, I remembered in turn how Martin would mock himself with Sir Galahad's boast: '*My strength is as the strength of ten because my heart is pure.*'

Even without assistance, Martin's heart beat on powerfully beneath his bony ribcage, for hour upon hour. Through that last night, as his body fought on, I kept reading the folk ballad he had translated, 'The Death of Dhiyenis', about the hero who had 'never feared a man among the brave'. Finally, however, Dhiyenis meets a stranger who challenges him to a contest of strength, 'and whichever should win would take the loser's soul'.

> And they went and wrestled on the marble threshing-floor;
> and where Dhiyenis struck the blood filled a trench,
> but where Death struck the blood filled a river.

When it was over, Roseanne and I went out onto the hospital forecourt. It was the dawn of the winter solstice.

Martin Johnston's sense of poetic timing was always perfect.

Acknowledgements

This book would not have happened without Vivienne Latham, née Bonney. The daughter of Roseanne Bonney, Vivienne was fifteen when Martin and Roseanne began living together. Martin loved his stepdaughter dearly, so it is fitting that Roseanne (who died in 2017) left the copyright in Martin's work to Vivienne. In 2019, Vivienne rang me and asked if I would be able to help her organise some sort of commemoration of the thirtieth anniversary of Martin's death, due in June 2020. This book is the result, together with a Martin Johnston memorial website: www.martinjohnstonpoet.com.

Vivienne and I would like to thank John and Lyn Tranter, whose enthusiasm and support for this whole commemorative project has been boundless. As well, both this selection and the website have been informed by *Martin Johnston, Selected Poems & Prose*, which John Tranter edited with selfless energy and devotion in 1993. Although that volume is out of print, Tranter's introduction—which includes information about Martin's life and publication history—is available on the Martin Johnston website, together with other material from the anthology.

Our thanks go, too, to Gig Ryan, a dear friend and colleague of Martin's, who over thirty years has continued to fly the flag for his work.

We thank Martin's brother, Jason, who has been a friend to both of us over many years.

For such a shy and private person, Martin had an extraordinary knack for friendship.

We acknowledge the ongoing loyalty and love of Martin's friends—poets, chess-players, former girlfriends, fellow-students and house-mates from university days, members of the Sydney Greek community, SBS colleagues ... Many of them have responded with great warmth to the prospect of this book, and the associated commemoration.

Sadly, Martin's friends in Greece tended to be so elderly that none are still alive, but a number of them are memorialised by name in this volume.

Finally, thanks to Ken Searle for the evocative cover illustration, to Wayne Davies for the cover photo, and to Matt Rubinstein at Ligature for his patience, his attention to detail, and his faith in this publication.

—N. W.

Selected Translations

from

Ithaka, Modern Greek Poetry in Translation

and

Martin Johnston, Selected Poems & Prose, ed. John Tranter

Pass By My Country

My friends of Roumeli, and you, sons of Moria,
by the bread we have eaten together,
by our brotherhood,
pass by my country and by my people.
Don't enter the village by sunlight
don't enter the village by moonlight
don't shoot your guns
don't sing your songs
for fear my mother might hear you, and my poor sister.
But if they come and ask you, the first time say nothing,
and if they doubly ask you, a second and a third time,
don't tell them I've been killed and make them sadhearted.
Just tell them that I've married here, here in these parts,
I have taken the grave for a mother-in-law,
the black earth for a wife,
and these strewn stones for my brothers and cousins.

—Anon

To Be a Kleft

If I could be a shepherd in May, a vinekeeper in August,
and in the heart of winter if I could be a wine-seller.
But better to be an armatol and a kleft,
an armatol in the mountains, a kleft in the plains,
have the rocks for brothers, the trees for relations,
sleep with the partridges, wake with the nightingales,
make my cross on the peak of Liakoura,
eat Turkish corpses, but not be called slave.

—Anon

The Death of Dhiyenis

Dhiyenis fights for his soul and the earth trembles.
The heavens roar and thunder, the upper world shakes,
the lower world is gaping, its foundations creak,
the tombstone shudders. How can it cover him,
cover the bold eagle of earth?
No roof could pen him in, no cave could hold him;
he strode over mountains, leapt over mountain peaks,
hurled great rocks, uprooted trees;
he caught birds in his hands, hawks on the wing,
running and leaping he caught wild goats and deer.

On Tuesday Dhiyenis was born, on Tuesday he will die.
He summoned all his friends to come, he summoned
    all the brave,
he called Minas and Mavrailis, he called the Ogre's Son,
he called on Tremandakheilos whom earth and heavens fear.
They came and found him lying on the plain.
He groaned and the mountains shuddered, groaned,
    and the valleys shook.
'What's come upon you, Dhiyenis? Why do you want to die?'
'Welcome, my friends, welcome, beloved friends.
Sit down and hold your peace and I shall tell you.
Through the mountains of Araby, through Syria's gorges
where two together dare not walk, nor three hold conversation,
but fifty and a hundred, and still they go in fear,
I passed alone, armed and on foot,
with my four-foot sword, with my three-fathom spear.

I crossed mountains and plains, mountains and gorges,
nights without starblaze, nights without moonlight.
And all these years I've lived here in the upper world
I've never feared a man among the brave.
But here I saw one barefoot and brightly clothed
who had the peacock's plumage and the lightning's eyes,
and he challenged me to wrestle him on the marble
   threshing-floor
and whichever should win would take the loser's soul.'
And they went and wrestled on the marble threshing-floor
and where Dhiyenis struck the blood filled a trench
but where Death struck the blood filled a river.

—Anon

The Witch

Black swallows from the wilderness,
white pigeons from the seashore,
as you fly high past my place,
nest in the apple-tree in my yard
and tell my dearest wife:
Let her marry, let her become a nun,
let her dye her clothes, let her wear black,
let her not wait for me or expect me.
For they've married me off here in Armenia
to an Armenian, a witch's daughter,
who enchants the stars and the sky,
enchants the birds so they don't fly,
enchants the rivers so they don't flow,
enchants the sea so it doesn't surge,
enchants the boats so they don't float
and enchants me so I don't come home.
When I set off there's rain and snow,
when I turn back, clear skies and sun.
I saddle my horse and it's unsaddled,
I gird on my sword and its ungirded,
I start to write and it's unwritten.

—Anon

Kitsos' Mother

Kitsos' mother sat on the bank of the river
and quarrelled with the river and stoned it.
'River, grow shallow! River, turn back!
so I can pass across to the kleft lairs
where the klefts are meeting, and all the chieftains.'

They have captured Kitsos and take him to be hanged.
A thousand go in front of him, two thousand behind,
and last, behind them all, goes his poor mother.
'My Kitsos, where are your arms? Where are your ornaments?
The five rows of buttons, your smoke-blackened buttons?'

'Mother, mad mother, stupid mother,
mother, don't you weep for my youth? Don't you weep
    for my strength?
Do you only weep for the miserable weapons, the blackened
    ornaments?'

—Anon

Old Horoscopes

Now don't you fret, Mr Sylvester, nothing wrong with the shop
though I won't say it's the best—pride before a fall and so on,
and besides, you never know what you're in for.
    But as I was saying,
I was born around the same time as plenty of others,
each of us due for something different. Some of us
    having to work,
others getting learning, or love, or being pious in monasteries,
or summer holidays by the sea or in the hills,
or the highest honours of state.
Anyway, Mr Sylvester, I turned out to be a boy, of course,
which pleased my parents no end. My father celebrated
by taking a couple of potshots at the rooftiles across the road,
and the trees (it was winter) kind of shone in the snow.
Everyone was happy and shouting, and he pulled
    the blinds back
and peered out at the first star he spotted—
actually it happened that only one was shining
at the time, the evening star as we call it.
He had this idea that he could bargain with the star,
maybe come to some agreement about my future;
who doesn't want his son to be a king? But,
well, Mr S., as you can see, I never did become a king
or anything of the sort.

True enough, I've turned out to be a good tradesman
with one of the best businesses in town. Even so—
if I could only ask that evening star to come down a bit closer
and make an appointment, over there beyond the last trees,
I'd skip the till for a while and ask it:
What was the arrangement? Did you take any notice
of my father's look, of my poor father's pleading gaze?

—Andhreas Karandonis

The Theft

One night
you'll hear a loud knocking
and it'll be the people
who've come with their real faces.
You'll open the door as though you expected it,
as though you weren't only eight years old.
They'll come in
and they'll be everyone:
enemies, strangers, friends.
You'll search their faces in vain
for a sign of regret.
You won't search.
Before they say a word you'll understand
so, quietly,
you'll take off your jacket
and give it to them,
take off your shirt
and give it to them,
don't let them take any trouble: guide them
as they take and take and take,
don't let them suspect that they haven't taken everything.
You can cry again
when at last they've finished
and go away, satiated.

—*Renos Apostolidhis*

Naxos

We set off for Naxos on April the nineteenth
by the regular Saturday afternoon steamer,
a crowd of private and public servants, embarking,
as I said, on Saturday afternoon,
paying God knows what for our passage.

We arrived after two hundred miles and maybe a dozen hours.
That is to say: we arrived
geographically speaking, or from what you might call
the ship's viewpoint, since after all
we'd squeezed every last inch out of our tickets ...
but no Naxos!
And yet the chart insisted
that this port was Naxos,
and all the townsfolk swore: Damn our souls,
they said, if this isn't Naxos
and we its inhabitants.

We left, disappointed in Naxos and its people.

If only the fools who met us at the quay had had the brains
to reject who they were, and where,
that might have been the Naxos that we'd hoped for.

—*Iakovos Kampanelis*

On Stage

1

You play with me sun
but this is no dance
so much nakedness
almost blood
or a wild wood;
then

2

Gongs, and the heralds.
I hadn't expected them,
had even forgotten their intonations.
Relaxed, freshly-clothed, bearing fruit-bowls.
I marvelled, whispering
that amphitheatres pleased me.
The shell filled at once,
the stage-lights dimmed
as for a renowned assassination.

3

You: what were you after? Your face contorted.
Just as you'd risen
leaving the cold sheets and the baths of vengeance.
Drops rolled down your shoulders,
your stomach, your bare feet
onto the reaped grass.
They, the three faces of bold Hekate.
They wanted to take you with them.
Your eyes two tragic seashells, on your breasts
the nipples cherry-coloured pebbles,
stage properties, I don't know ...
they howled, you remained rooted,
their gestures ripped at air.
Slaves brought their knives
and you remained a rooted cypress.
They drew the knives from their sheaths
looking for a place to strike you.
And only then you cried
'Let whoever likes bed me!
Am I not the sea?'

4

The sea, how did the sea become so?
For years I tarried in the mountains
blinded by fireflies.
Now, on this shore, I wait
for a man to moor,
flotsam, a raft.

But can the sea be infected?
A dolphin gashed it once
and once a gull's wingtip.

Yet the waves were sweet
when as a child I leapt in them and swam
when as a youth
I pieced out patterns in the pebbles
looking for rhythms
the Old Man of the Sea said to me:
'I am your country,
I may be no-one
but I can be what you want.'

5

Who heard at midday
the knife sliding across the whetstone?
What horseman came
with torch and kindling?
Who disembowelled
the woman the child and the house?
No-one's guilty; gone into smoke.
Who rode away,
hooves clattering across the paving-stones?
They have abrogated sight, they're blind,
there are no longer any witnesses.

6

When will you speak again?
Our words are many men's children.
They're sown they're born like children
they take root they feed on blood.
As pine trees hold the wind's form
after the wind's gone, is no longer there,
so words preserve man's form
and he's gone, he's no longer there.
Perhaps the stars want to speak
that walked across your nakedness one night,
Cygnus Sagittarius Scorpio,
perhaps those.
But where will you be at the moment
when light comes to this theatre: here?

7

Yet there on the other shore
under the stars of the black cave
suns in your eyes birds on your shoulders
you were there; suffering
the other pain, love
the other dawn, the presence
the other birth, resurrection;
yet there you became again
in time's vast diastole
moment by moment like resin,
stalactite, stalagmite.

—*George Seferis*

Drinking 'Sans Rival' Ouzo

Drinking 'Sans Rival' ouzo
I thought of the ancient fields, unfinished phrases
of olives or lentils or a little cheese from Kythnos.
The way the basement smelt
and the toilet key, always in the landlord's hands.
Stratos, Prokopis, Kostas, Vayas from upcountry
who came to town to become a film director,
friends who can no longer drink, or now drink without me.

And I remembered it all
like a Cavafy poem in translation
when the original's been lost.
Unable at last to cope with the graze of memory
you add ice and water, and drink a liquid
white, nostalgic and serene.

—*Vassilis Vassilikos*

Elegy

God will have smiled some time in your eye's fire
spring will have locked her heart in the pearl
   of an ancient shore

Now as you sleep shining
on the frozen plain where the wild vines
become embalmed feathers marble pigeons
dumb children of expectation—

I wanted you to come one evening like a welling cloud
stonespray olivedust
because some time
I too would have seen on your pure forehead
the snow of sheep and lilies
but you passed from my life like a tear of the sea
like a summer firefly like May's last rain
Though you too were once a geranium-coloured wave
a bitter pebble
a little swallow in a deserted forest
with no bell at dawn with no lamp at evening
with your warm heart turned far away
to the ruined teeth of the other shore
to the shattered islands of the wild cherry and the seal

—Nikos Gatsos

Selected Poems

from

shadowmass

The Sea-Cucumber

The Typewriter Considered as a Bee-Trap

and

Martin Johnston, Selected Poems & Prose, ed. John Tranter

To Greece Under the Junta

No bird sang that year
save the bitter partridge,
nor on dark slopes
thyme nor basil grew.
Sheepbells then were waterfalls
of liquid brass, clouds
dropping from glass dawns.
The prickly pear's grip
enfolded ancient stones of fading patterns.

After the massacre of the goats
yellow eyes peer from high crevices,
wink from the scuttering lizard.
Old Typhon scrambles
belching from Etna.

Flowers and sulphur
and the gap-toothed prophet
capers among the gullies.

Do not enter the village
by sunlight or by moonlight.

In Memoriam Phan Thi Mao

if this were a poem I might have said that
wars kill their living (of course more
lyrically), that there is finally
nothing to say (& said it), that
'every bird ... is an immense world of delight', or spoken
of the sudden carnation of death.

but because this is not a poem
suffice it to say that phan thi mao who was
so it was said at the autopsy
18 to 20 and of mongolian racial stock
was dragged into a hillside shelter
fucked by four american soldiers
shot from the front &
bayoneted from behind

> 'it was just like when you
> stick a deer with a knife—
> sort of thud—or
> something like
> this, sir'

I am sick of perfecting my technique
O for a civilisation of dolphins

Undergrowth

for Sarah

in a curving season   when the morning glory
strangled the papyrus in our garden
nuzzling the gentle bruise   with leper tenderness
I wore the embrace of bindweed

as earth tumbled & I opened to the sun
leaves quested at another pore   delicately
feathered flesh   caressing inward
seeding in the cavities of bone

kelp-coloured light flowered across my brain
orchids spored under green bottle glass
heavy planets   swirling to mandragora
hunkered in eyesockets

& reaching down through the chill fingers
carried me like a tatty overcoat
into a night of hamadryads   asking
a dust of pollen only   knotted bark inside

recoiled at evening   moss & lichen stooped
my tongue to rank declivities of soil
refracting speech with dayfall   foliage
coiled & humping

we were a small wrinkled asteroid
lurching in emerald down the night
until air became space   & all the flowers
withering unchoked our lips

with dawn   but we had both dreamed
of an enormous iridescent fish
swimming   black & yellow
among leaves in the pearled roads of Newtown

& of snails on a broken caryatid
so that when we were speaking
it was to grow the morning glory
out of our eyes again   in a curving season

Sequestrum

There's a special sort of madness in the colours
beyond the spectrum: not infra-red
but the colours of shapes around the corners
of fogged-up glasses when, in the evening,
trees are faint white networks through the sky.
Perhaps the cat at least knows them,

not our cat, of course, but some impossible
Osiris sun-cat with convolvulus ears; or
dry desires might stir the worm's path
over a different road.
To us are decreed only
wings that dilate in memory
where houses whirled around the skyline,
thunder of clapping winds, nightshade in nightshade.

But the cat makes passes, feints
at those pale fruit like fishbowls, or the curlew
chimes on the belltower, rattles at the window.
Birdlime and aspic, golden nets to catch the time:
here is no inland sea.

To the Great Anger of the Nubians

Anno 1670, not far from Cyrencester, was an Apparition. Being demanded, whether a good Spirit or a bad? returned no answer, but disappeared with a curious Perfume and a most melodious Twang.

—John Aubrey, *Miscellanies*

I think the sarcophagus of Seti I
shared the front parlour with a stuffed gorilla.
The attendants were noted for their courtesy.
Six, in a blue duffle coat,
I climbed on the proscenium and remember
a Japanese flower unfolding
in the distilled and tasteless past.

When Pythagoras ate black beans, and had nearly finished,
he put one on each side of the plate, so that
with one lunge and guzzle he could say
Look, a dot in a circle, if at all
anything, no guilt of mine;
so love and strife contended.
But I knew nothing of Seti or Pythagoras.

'I the magnificent Belzoni
six foot seven in my viridian stockings
stamped on the stuffed and dead
my own new currency of fortitude.

When I sat down
I snapped mummies under me like bandboxes.
I've seen dangling in the webs of certain spiders
just such matrices as these ... as though
the blueprint is at last drawn up
when the building is again loam;
so I thought at Abu Simbel.
For my own part, I am content
although I stink a little still
of elephant piss and sawdust.'

A sweet and personable chaos
inviting unregenerate dust
was seen (in the Sir John Soane museum) wobbling one morning
out of a boarded window.
Recognised as such,
if only, then, by P.C. Ramdas Singh,
it was promptly dragged back into its box
where, the night-watchman said,
it muttered threnodies in quarter-tones
greatly disconcerting a passing rapist.

Gorillas don't go Bong. People do.
If an old southerly
feathers the cranium with caressing rain,
some turnip-footed yokel in Italian shoes
will warp your raindrop into gullies
irrigating someone's cornflakes,
squash beetles on the counterpane,
if he can cast a memory theatre
(Giordano Bruno didn't have this in mind)
with his own harlequins and cucumbers; and so piranhas starve
in arid Amazons of sludge.

'I Sir John Soane, an architect of note,
threw an all-night party
after acquiring the sarcophagus of Seti I
thanks to the intrepid Giovanni Belzoni.
Will some woodsman
sell me Yggdrasil at last?—
he can cut it down if necessary.
Think of my bequest:
I wear confusion like a carapace.'

One with the steps
I funnelled into finepoint
past at web's edge.
Years later I read that spider filament
'is the second strongest substance extant
after fused quartz' whatever that is.
And later again that spiders on acid
weave Jackson Pollocks.
But the enshrouded pharaoh had dripped his juice
and all contingencies had merged
in a consummation of dry grass
and a splintered waterhole.

Form into form anarchic evening
pokes halberds through the futtered eyeholes
of a dying city.

'I the geomancer of Yunnan province
drank overmuch the yellow rice wine
(justly celebrated) of this district. Consequently
hauled befuddled to the ceremony
I placed the auspicious moment stone
slightly at an angle. Now these three thousand years
nothing has happened in this city of T'eng-yueh
except that everything has gradually grown drier

and that here plagues are born; therefore
soon they are going to build another
(also, I understand, at a slight angle).
But I went down to the sea;
roiled in kelp and sea-kale
to the shark's gullet, finally
down to the charitable plankton.
Aromatic, I shall soon arise
steaming from bouillabaise or chowder
and claim my dispensation;
although no-one remembers my name any longer
and I myself have lost it in some fish's maw.'

Orion rolls in the sky's gut
and the jerky fingers of silence between spaces
bounce a ball of husk.

Spinoza

Spinoza scratched a core of light
assimilating all perceived
and thrust its splinters in his eyes
dust where existence interleaved

the trees that filtered down the square
could only spike the circle's rim
with arclit equidistant points
parameters of seraphim

Spinoza cycles upside-down
around his attic torture-track
scrawling moustaches on God's face
extinguishing the zodiac

and pedals madly till the wheel
must grope for spinning's last extreme
and floats out past the asteroids
nobody's halo no one's dream

Letter to Sylvia Plath

i.m. C.C.

I

Impacted fans of dawn unfold
aubades of memory. Through the street
cat-eyed last night's now stirring, curled
across the window, round your feet.

Worlds' whirling: cellos in the fur
will scrape the brain across a string
unfurling spiderwebs in air
to suck the discords mornings bring

when evenings twitter and grow stale.
The game's musical cats. The prize,
a peepshow glimpse at what you fail,
or come too late to realise

of nights. You'll notice, though the wine
sheened you in canopies of gold,
the glitter's trickled down to stain
the morning's floor. It's hot (it's cold).

II

'You're wearing yourself again.'
The fragile occupant recalls
flowering of emblematic veins
to foliate paper on the walls

which are all acting's foliage.
Then consciousness assumes a place
where memory theatre marks the stage;
rooting against the carapace

tendrils gone mandrake writhe and slide
because a nerve refracted there
touches their filigree's outside
and makes a scream out of thin air.

The walls grow rot and fungi pass
from smell to form. The patrons come,
crumble to waterfalls of glass.
Pale eyes from the proscenium.

The Sea-Cucumber

for Ray Crooke

We'd all had a bit too much that night when you brought out
    your painting,
the new one, you remember, over Scotch in the panelled kitchen,
and my father talked about waiting. Well, he was doing that,
    we knew,
or it could have been the dust you'd painted, the way
    you'd floated
a sfumato background almost in front of the canvas
so your half-dozen squatting dark figures couldn't see it
that moved him in that moment softly, in damp stone,
    outside time.
He was as garrulous as ever, of course, but somehow,
in a time of his own, it seemed that he was pressing
every word-drop, like the wine of a harvest not quite adequate,
to trickle in brilliant iridules across the stained table:
what sorts of eucalypt to plant—so that they'd grow quickly—
art dealers, metaphysics, three old men he'd seen
at Lerici, playing pipes and a drum under an orange sky.
Memory finds a nexus, there in your image,
people just waiting, not even conscious of it,
or of ochre and sienna pinning them in an interstice of hours.
None of this, you see, will really go into writing,
it takes time to leech things into one's sac of words.

The bloated sea-cucumber, when touched, spews up its entrails
as though that were a defence; my father's old friend
the gentle little poet Wen Yi-tuo, who collected chess sets
and carved ivory seals in his filthy one-room hut,
is gutted one night and flung into the Yangtze.
The dark river runs through your dusty pigments.
Ferns, moss, tiger-coloured sun beat at the window with banners
but the dust ripples between trees, and among the waiting
glints of earth and metal are wiped from the fading hand.
These people of yours, Ray, they are that evening
when we first saw them, or the other one when my father
planted nineteen saplings in our backyard, or when you looked
    at them
later and said, They're coming on, and his fingers
drummed a long nervous question on the table, though
    he agreed.
And we were all waiting, though not in your style of art:
more of a pointillism in time, disconnected moments,
a flash of light over an empty glass, a half-finished volume
    of Borges,
the cabbage palm stooping at dusk into the chimneys,
certain paintings, Corelli, or a morning like the fuzz
    of a peach,
all bright and disparate. But I think, remembering that painting
of yours, that if one could step away, ten yards, or twenty,
    or years,
at an angle perhaps, a frame would harden into cedar
and through a haze of dust we would see all the brilliant dots
merge into a few figures, squatting, waiting.

Mazurka for Buzzing Fly

(Grand master Akiba Rubinstein speaks)

Lost in glass gullies, searching for a suitcase ...
—David Campbell

The spectacles perched on my brain
guard its moist shadows from the sun
that creeps like acid down the walls
of this hotel room, in a town
I'll leaved unnamed, for fear
the masters of the buzzing fly may hear.
Safe for a moment, I'll explain.
My father gave me dust, bad eyes, the law,
the golden letters of the Name
at tunnel's end, and turned me out
into talmudic dark.
The white-tipped cane he gave me
was to be pointed only, not to guide, and so
reproach became escape, escape pursuit,
a thing I found out later when I died.
Sometimes I think that I've become a planet
and through the cold blue light
of my made space, by squinting I can see
where my perspectives end
a distant point of gold, a knifetip-bright
sun towards which my ellipses ache to bend.

Except this insect, hovering around
my head, scratching at nerve-ends with its sound,
its endless whining, has suborned my sight.
I've filled this room with mirrors:
full-length, distorting, compact, shaving-glasses,
serried around the walls and on the ceiling.
Nothing that passes
can pass unseen. I have a feeling
that there's another head behind my head,
or else the fly is also dead.
I can no longer think.
Master Alekhine lost himself in drink,
and crabbed old Steinitz played a game with God
by cordless invisible telephone,
and Schlechter, the frail little Viennese
starved to death quietly in a room like this:
they weren't the same. I drove to the bone
of this our murderous game,
they called me the Spinoza of the chessboard.
And now I bolt the door
and peer for flyshit on the floor.
Not far from here Spinoza faced the mob.
I could still trace my last Rook line,
out of this room, into the city square:
the glib voluptuaries of the mind
could finish off their job. But I'll not save them time.
All's curved and soft, my thought
is overripe and rotting. If I could stop that fly,
if I could stop that fly: here I'd remain
hearing once more the crystal music of my brain.

Gradus Ad Parnassum

for David Campbell

Over a tabasco sandwich, with black coffee
and a number of cigarettes ('one of my breakfasts')
I've been rereading a poem about *The Shipwreck
of the Heart*, or some such—the title isn't important,
only, of course, the Image—by the well-known
Russian revolutionary poet Vladimir Mayakovsky.
This he wrote immediately before indulging
in the uncharacteristic excess of suicide;
the poem, perhaps because of this, is peculiarly flabby
for this normally vigorous author, is, how shall I put it,
    sentimental.
Of course he never had a chance to revise it.
So, having nothing better to do at the moment,
    and in accordance
with my (borrowed) idea that we're all one writer
and ought, in any case, to do one another justice,
I thought I might have a go at it
on his behalf. I like to think he wouldn't mind,
though he did once call Dante and Petrarch tongue-tied.

One way of approaching it would be what I'd call the Arnoldian
(cf. The Scholar-Gypsy)—the extended thalassic metaphor,
the tang of myth, the vague yearning (perhaps *tristesse*
is more or less the word) after something or other indefinable.
But it would be hard not to be woolly.

Seferis could get away with that sort of thing; but he's a Greek,
in this, as in other lines of business, an advantage.
I don't think it'll do.
Or perhaps something after the manner of Rimbaud,
Le Bateau Ivre, say. It's been done, I grant you
—there's a new Rimbaud every week or so—but it does offer
both astringency and lots of freedom. It's tempting;
and I could invoke Hoffmansthal too, and his incredible boat
'with enormous yellow sails', the ideal dreamscape property
if ever there was one.
Except Rimbaud never had to face
that particular situation; it was always poor Verlaine
who copped it—court cases, absinthe, all very sordid—
     and *his* style,
I'm sure of it, would be worse than useless.

A good line (ironic distancing) would be the cheerfully morbid
surrealist—black comedy, kitsch, *fantastically* rich
imagery—the sort of thing David Campbell does so well
in his latest book. I mean, you could have these merchants,
whores, and sailors gaping on this picturesque waterfront
as this bloody great red, pulsating thing comes in
beating past the headlands, with Joe the little cabin boy
sticking his head out of the aorta to be sick.
And then Whoompf! the reef, and Squelch! the blood,
with the sun opportunely setting. I mean, it's powerful ...
but just a little ... heavy-handed? And critics seem to think
that's all passé. Dr Tiptoes
wouldn't take it seriously. You can't win.

Or, again, the nebulously cosmic: a giant uvula
suddenly becoming discernible on the skyline—
shades of Fenrir at Ragnarok—
teeth poking through the clouds, a crunching sound,
end, but *end*, of poem. But I've done very similar things

myself, earlier on. I don't want to end up in self-parody,
I know too many critics. And I've been a little unkind
myself, perhaps, on occasion. It would hardly be politic.

And the groovier modern Americans? They seem to be
    the context
I'm supposed to work in, though I mostly haven't read them.
But their thing about the quotidian, and the earth,
and the immanence of the tremendous in just about everything—
what kind of immanence is left for something tremendous?
Like an extravagant outsized Russian
about to do himself in, shat with love and the party?
What has that to do with the grass? Tenochtitlan?
    Cotton Mather
or your friend and fellow-poet who happened to drop in?

.... and one is left, it seems to me, with the techniques
    and words
of Vladimir Mayakovsky, who wrote this poem,
The Shipwreck of the Heart or whatever, just before
shooting himself, if I remember rightly.
I'm not sure that it's much of a poem
but it'll have to do. I'm thirsty to start with
and the pubs have opened, and besides I think deep down
    I'm hoping
that someone will try to pinch *my* poems, and much good
may it do them: each one the precise, the only possible
delineation of a complex of thinking and feeling;
the explanation of each poem
precisely the poem itself.
Sometimes it's hard to repress a snigger. Still, a beer
and buy the papers and some more tabasco
and maybe another bash at Mayakovsky ......

Fault Line

One might be happier if they were less banal
in their coming. The least you'd expect is talons
or the odd fang, something like sudden orchids
and a scuttling behind the crockery in the half-light.
Sundew, amanita
muscaria, Venus flytrap, gauds among pages
of moist pulp, mouthless where no insects fly,
cringe on our side of the smoked brittle glass
from the crones' quickening wings.
The years have been hard on the indifferent Furies.
The best they can do an epileptic girl
tossing on broken bottles in our alley, literary, implausible.
The best they want to do. Nobody takes hints
these days; they live for a voyeur at a broken mirror.
To see a poem
the man in the back row puts on his glasses.
His pupils carome up, socketed egg-whites
bind the fluttering hall in a web of shadow.
He stuck a pin into each bulb. Wet light
seethed through the holes. Corroding, we swam through our
    own eyes
while through the pane those bored old fabulators
fingered us for a moment wistfully like silk
and coiled back sucking, damp with love:
in spring the coy bloodflowers question the welcoming air.

The Blood Aquarium

> On one walk he 'gave' to me each tree we passed, with the reservation that I was not to cut it down or do anything to it, or prevent the previous owners from doing anything to it: with those reservations it was henceforth mine.
>
> —Norman Malcolm, *Ludwig Wittgenstein: A Memoir*

> They do not apprehend how being at variance it agrees with itself; there is a back-stretched connection, as in the bow and the lyre.
>
> —Herakleitos

1

Pan Apolek's scarf whirls the horizon inward,
he brittle and void inside its tightening belt.
The wet sky's writhing flings scurf among the branches,
mist banners over churned soil.
The blind man's fingers
caress an accordion like a skull.
Palette and paint flow into the mountain,
the mountain flows through the painter.
Toppling from high cliffs, he falls
into himself, and is eaten:
a starting point.

2

Han-shan: 'The Cold Mountain'.
Sandalwood night smokes through liquid pines,
stars dissolve in water to a whitish powder.
The skin if heated can be broken with a blunt knife;
inside will be found
small galaxies drifting flat against the eyes
listen   they can be either
stapled or glued together
                         calm   a place of calmness
                         the infested body
is brittle as old paper
or is
smells yellow as sandalwood,
nebulae rotate in grains across the cornea,
grit into words:
                         stars are serrated are bright heavy teeth
                         the skin can be broken can be cracked
keeping still
says the I Ching keeping his back still   so that
he no longer feels his body
he goes into the courtyard and does not see his people.
No blame.

Keeping still is the mountain
(swansneck night inhales the brain
fading to gnarled negative
                         in the lightroom of smoke
                                     leaf fingered night
inhales and flows)   I was born,
says the defunct Aztec, on the mountain. No one
becomes a mountain no one
turns himself into a mountain
                         the mountain crumbles

3

'There is no riddle' / moon flute   moon bone   ice bone

Sentences coil out of a flux of blindworms,
arc out of flow to freeze
flow into words' envenomed husk.

To extract cubes place tray under warm water,
then even a blunt knife will do.

4

The tension of the erect bowstring pertains to silence
that of the senses to Cold Mountain's tigers.
Light rilling into the eyes unnoticed
skitters down the brain in mossdark shadows;
raddled in the guts of a fanged wanting
rivers beat at tunnels,
things drinking into these words
burst torrents against the skin, rainbows in froth
spattering seep to pagination
                                          or the archer's hand
slips, or relaxes.

5

Nolan once tipped up a Riverina landscape
to see if its lakes would drip to the warehouse floor.
Paddling and lapping, we consider fountains,
how, if they came together,
each pair of drops would meet and leap apart: salto,
and a third sphere dancing unseen between the others.
Peddling topologies of doubt, damp fingers
touch fountain and lip,

draw over a voluptuary tongue the graph
of curves immeasurably lost: though the tall-thighed typists
whinny and click still across the pavements
we prick over coffee to light's gay acupuncture,
plot our own drowning
under the equivocal benedictions of the sun.

6

Han-shan: 'The Cold Mountain'.
Pascal squats here, muttering for a duster,
and Evariste Galois bursts in the cold red dawn
and becomes an inkblot;
              scanning we may, yes, plot the tangents of night

And in the thirtieth century before Christ
Fu Hsi invents the binary system;
shamans and rancid lamas
festoon their greasy scalps with the bones of thought
and waggle their heads at the moon and the snow.
The Sixty-Four Diagrams
invoke Maitreya, the Buddha who is to come.
    Keeping still is the mountain, but there are modes of stillness,
    as the flight of eagles silver against soaring thunder
    or the fall from high places when the mountain drops.

Along the slippery ledges of the body
one sometimes finds abandoned middens
in old caves and scrapings, where only fragile ferns
or moss offer a foothold; fall
into a dream of green twilight forests
where every leaf is known in love and name.

      the mountain
      crumbles

7

Flux is a nounless language. Thinking 'it moons',
'it saffrons', words caper down the nerves
to burst in aureoles at the fingertips.
Lights out and the room swims.
Angler fish, Roman candle,
immortal crepuscular verb.

8

The track there veers through the fir cones,
balances on the sharp edge of morning,
skirts the streams frozen into fingers
and snow filtering through pine needles' gauze.
The aquarium floats in cool green air
etching its images hard against glass walls.
Bulbous shapes fishing night's abysses
trail points of light, drift across dreams,
bend out of shape and burst as the pressure ebbs:
nonchalant sneak thief, I saunter across the walkways,
amble past the tanks where light creaks
and siphon it off into my font. The fishtails whip
and curl against the sun. Flattening, they excite
the cracking of night's last pale porcelain.
Dawn's knife hacks at the sky's belly
reddening cloudruns through the tanks; the guts
bubble through the blood aquarium.
Plate glass flows into filigrees of pine,
oxygen tubes squirm bleeding
across carmine snow.
                                      Clocks, newspapers,
fish and attendants, peanut wrappers
become rubber and liquid, stifle. Concrete plugs the senses,
forces the mouth open, sears the palate,

rasps at the back of the eyeballs; the tide rises.
Spiralling currents lash at pine-trunks.
Past Santorini and Krakatoa the whiskered hermits
paddle by, sulphurous, on mushrooms.
The observer gobbles blood and ink,
stone, scarlet stone, rubies and porphyry,
red stone for images and typeface
grinding runes in a blind language.
On a stained scrap written
the smell of some inevitable jasmine flower
buried in dawn?

9

Vogelfrei:
a merry-go-round with claws.
                          An expression has meaning
                          only in the stream of life
                          (so Wittgenstein)
when with the Galway foxhounds he would ride
and fling himself along the pentachord
of whistling's orbit. The kite of his silence
hangs through a hole in air,
aspiring to the condition of music.
Hunted carrion bird, backyard abortionist,
scalpelling liquid droppings from the brain,
sculpting
the stasis of the photographed sonata.
His eyes are washed pebbles.

10

Set apart end of this talking:
not Bercilak or a black gale,
crunch of snapping sea-rocks,
rather a multiple exposure. First
sheathed copper cuirass and greaves
a spidering figure of black iron
hulks moonskinned in mantis posture, blowtorching the brain:
the ritual suicide of a foreign race.
The mountain grasses
have sap like milk or semen,
they wave around rotting helmets
on the rock slabs, beaten by the sun's brass shield.
Scavenging children gather tissues gone liquid
in small cooking pots.
Green poet soup:
'Something he ate that disagreed with him.'
Conosco i segni dell' antica fiamma.

11

Walking home one night, under a streetlamp,
I came upon a man without a nose.
                          What struck me, at the time, as sad
was that I was reminded of Gogol: so, I thought,
even your compassion stinks of libraries.
His eyes were quite gentle and puzzled as he just stood there
and I walked on nervously, although nothing had happened.
But what if his nose had just dropped off
a moment before, and he was cradling it in his handkerchief
uncertain whether to call the police or the doctor,
or whether to trust a passing stranger?

Perhaps as I looked at him, if I'd stayed,
his ears would have plopped into the gutter,
his toes skittered and bounced playfully across the damp street,
and, in short, all of him come unstuck.
What if all that was left,
hovering at eye level as he fell apart,
was a piece of notepaper
with something written on it in a foreign language?
And I went away without trying to read it
because the alley cats were munching his eyeballs?

12

Rain slices the night,
moonstalks lick around wet leaves.
Whales and sea-snakes drift through the branches,
striping the shadows with cold colour.
The sky chipped bone over woods' rustling.

Squatting in a black clearing flecked on the foothills
someone is trying to light a match.

13

                                      'All in the not done,
all in the diffidence that faltered.'

Conversely,
there's being in a bone-coloured room in a white house
at the convergence of several roads
with images of a kind of desperation
that may not even be one's own; perhaps typing,
unawares, the uncreating word.

Or eaten from the inside
by all the manic net of the senses trawled
or the gangster mind spraying slugs and acid.

I wonder if the statistician's fortunate ape
after the last page of the First Folio
knew itself as more than punctuation
emphasising inaudible harmonies,
intonations of a forgotten speech.
                                    Had Easter Island an epic poem?

14

Green and gold, a girdle scarfs the sky's edge
around porcelain enamelled green to purple
glittering with reflected forests. Lying in the middle
of the jewelled world Gwalchmai, sun-hawk,
dreams of pterodactyls that stew in the mud
mulching livid gobbets in gaunt beaks.

In his golden halo
flapping through citrus groves, backward
where the swamp creeps up on him along the shadows
grapnelling his taildown's sweep and rush
with trellises of baobab and magnolia
and giant ferns squatting in the sunlight,
o mud bubbles finely where the swift curve
of his wingtips brushes over air glaze
into slate with a toothed screech.

15

Early morning on the Cold Mountain;
fog skeins the frosted grass
and the archaeologists are scrambling up the cliff-face
with tape-measures and little hammers.
Eyes blearing through salt mist
they gavotte upwards, tapping each other's heads
or sketching their own eyes on ruled notepaper.
Someone cracks a cloudbank:
sand ruffle by basalt seas:
the mountain slides, twitching.
       The peak flops over,
the stone archaeopteryx
sunning itself under a transparent umbrella
is betrayed by a toothy grin
in a toothpaste earthquake.
Click and buzz,
the fossickers pop off;
     and the knight in the enker grene
     whiderwardeso-ever he wolde.
The shield with its endless knot
clumps down and squashes the lot.

16

Curtained in claret hessian
my window is usually open.
I tend to wake up late, and sometimes people
throw peaches or grapefruit through the window.
When the pubs close
swollen faces pass like leprous asteroids.
They'd knock on the window if it were closed;
air, I've found, is the best obstacle.
Air makes thick, rich glass: at some point in the house
light filtered through our many curtains meets
unseen in a dance of colours; so, turned in lamplight,
we live in an old bottle.
Just before dawn one glimpses the cellarmen:
little knots of cut glass statues
huddling and whispering in the dusty wind,
tinkling in vans' headlights
in these concentric, faded vaults
in the stomach of the mountain we fell in to.
When it drizzles pepsin the lady down the road
clutches her grey hair, scuttling
between the garbage can and her carnations.
But, floating under a blood-coloured light bulb,
we mull into punch the rendered tissues of our keepers,
toast glass in glasses shot with streaks of red.
I think of hawks snapping in the invisible sky
with a frightened mutation of pity.

17

                                      the mountain crumbles
keeping still is the mountain   a peaceful place
among trees   it is a place of
peace
a tree place,   among trees
a place of terror

                              no one
                              becomes a mountain
                              almost

18

Tonight the air is delicate
like those tremulous aquatints
in the better Victorian chronicles of travel.
One would expect it to lisp.
'I think I would look better,' it might say,
'in basic black.'
And in the night's night
we swing on the clapper of a black bell, tolling
impossible polyphonies of burnished fish
into the squittering plasma that surrounds us.
We're played on a xylophone of coral.
Until deferential morning sidles up:
'The sort of place I had in mind' (coughing discreetly)
'is not unlike that depicted
on a packet of Alpine; the colours are more or less right
and "fresh filtration" conveys, I feel,
something of the appropriate idea.'

19

The Celestial Stag
according to Jorge Luis Borges
inhabits deep tunnels in Manchuria.
It is so named
because of its ambition
to rise to the surface
and the sky,
                              upon doing which
it turns immediately into a foul odour.
This is recounted in a volume entitled
The Book of Imaginary Beings.

20

'The colour transmitted
is always complementary to the one reflected.'

'Green and gold came together
in a dancing instant of white light.
All the air grained with pollen,
the flowers translucent, moss whispering through my fingers,
the moon arching like a stroked kitten
as in the peace of this small room
from which I can see neither moon nor flowers
I stroke violet petals of air;
the fuzz bees left covers my eyelids.
Hair incandescent with a sprinkling of meteors
some time I could
feel over my naked feet
the stir and rustle of the dancing water
that is more than water, in the cool silver stream
that weaves in separate strands
its thin music on a fragile mountain

hidden in jasmine-scented clouds.
Hidden in a point of light, the mountain
where the rivers were written by Corelli.'

21

Shut down shop, hang the willow-pattern,
cage its bouncing monks with rough slats.
Put your head on a potter's wheel,
spin life backwards in clay rivulets,
sink into fine china. Grass grows
pale blue, the colour of baptism:
shuffle the hill people, strung on a stalk:
press them into the clay as the wheel whirls faster,
until all the figures coalesce
at the consistency of a cooked eye;
this is what is known as the science of optics.
Roll them into a ball, turn round in a circle
looking at the horizon. And I became quite dizzy
with turning, looking for just the slightest indentation
in the sky's perfect hemisphere.
Only a bird hung silent above me,
too far to distinguish colour or kind.
There are holes ripped in the paper plain,
already my ankles have gone through the surface.
I'd like to see, while I have time,
where that bird has got to: but everything has become a funnel
and only a scream curves down
from the place high above where the bird is drowning
in the purity of the air that shapes it.
A needle pokes through the top of the sky,
the conical sky, the sky shaped like the inside of a mountain.

And a little old Chinese leaps worriedly
out of his plate, and with his palsied hands
tears up pieces of paper, chews them, spits up the pulp,
frantically building up small heaps covered with tigers.
He falls through. No, there he is,
so high one can hardly see him,
vanishing into the funnel's mouth.
The boys are waiting round the corner; time to shut down
    for the day.

22

And the quarry, pinned in a sapless tussock,
feels itself shredding around the arrowhead,
nerves twisting from the sharp intimacy of steel.
With the bowstring's twang and release, the archer
flows over the abrading ground into the victim's eye.
Clasped together they watch the sun go dim.

On the Zeeland shore a whale rots, waiting for Dürer.
Saffron shrouds the foaming cliffs,
golden bells underneath await their cracking; and every twig
of the dour trees near the snowline
turns into a flute, rolling the sun along
until he splashes drunken among the islands.

My curtain has stepped aside.
In the street are the throb of trucks, and children running,
and what I think are sparrows pecking around the hubcaps.
No offence taken, none intended:
a brightly coloured interval in air
why should I punctuate air's own provenance?

The spray of winefalls patters against the fish tanks
in a clearing where wooden statues genuflect
although dazzled by white light from the broken glass.
Around their rooted feet sift sheets of paper,
drenched and illegible. Someone has tacked up:
'Danger. The fish have escaped from the blood aquarium.'

23

The statues in the Parthenon used to be painted.
Painter and painting move
from jewelled ikons to sketches in wash and pen.
Brushing myself in
I try, still, not to tear the paper;
eating oneself is unseemly
and all these words have teeth like hungry rivers.

Moriarty at Reichenbach

I squat here under the falls waiting
for the Billygoats Gruff. My sodden fingers
pluck still a dropping harp. In the hotel
the pink skiers mumble in their dreams
and are puzzled at quarrels.
I've quirked to moss,

tried out cryptogamous disciplines
waiting for the thin hero. Motif
of the champion. These asteroids of mine
troll in fiddle music over the water.
Yes, I've spored
a stain in the wallpaper, obstinate

unfactorable equations.
I've squirmed fat salmon through my palms, patted them
upstream barbed with messages.
They tumble back in foam skewered
on the Guarneri. Counterthemes, unplanned intervals,
embarrassed pauses: catgut.

Wet grass, discoloured brick. The harp's
more honour. No middlemen.
We're changing places. In the twilit
plasma dancing between the cities
our nightly duet wakes
a station-master in the West of England

and a film of windmills and it starts. This pettiness!
Air's clear here, though, seeds
spread. Feel the familiar ripples.
I rose under the nonexistent bridge
in the mouth of the airgun barrel;
I need him rather less than he needs me.

Critical Notes on Marcel Proust

Rain slaps the bridge and the sea tilts. Water gathers
in a still fullness of curves. We screech on into the funnel
of sliding night, and the sky's melting
swallows us whole in its jellyfish umbrella.
The sea pours in and rusts our radio.
Our brains are become sponges in the sea's crannies
sifting chill water. Cells of remembrance
slurp wet at their begetting.
The music is in the water. Cilia whip out
at our castoff shadows whining across the surface.
Here occasions like worn coins present themselves
to suggest the memory of some transaction
of tears or kisses or music glistening
under another ocean or on a different bridge:
'PT ... M .. H.LOP ... R' or 'love' or a whistled pattern
of familiar notes from an unfamiliar song
without currency. We wave in the sea's rhythm, and suck in
water, and suck in water, and suck
in water

Cave

> Tartar here, Tartar there,
> in the darkness everywhere.
> Sleep my baby, sleep my bairn,
> Tartar comes for other men.
>
> —Old lullaby

Sharp mornings on railway stations
before the limeflower flutter of first light,
brackish mornings, lemon and rocksalt
in the wind's wake under blue ice
glitter, the slow glacier of stars.
My coat wrinkling dun against the silver
of mirroring elms and streetlamps, giraffes
eating in tall silence
night like a safety pin: a pure scream
of living glass pierces the suburbs:
dawn and the train.

Half-men fanned embers and beat sticks
waiting for the anachronistic dragon
gasping mouthfuls of sodden wood, snow,
whirling crystal lizards around the cavemouth,
there are relics.
The warm Aegean painted zodiacs of green fire
on our bodies when I was a child at night
the tinderbox moon struck sapphires like a mad forger

(no one swam past the quiet island
thirty yards out where nothing rippled).
Sprawled on the rocks we discussed ice,
atavism, rustling grass, fingernails
webbing the earth in dance just underground.
A girl stirred and the constellations
in her mail of seadrops became needles
rushing down tunnels of indigo, headlights
in cold rain, in veering night.
Stations are where the lines converge
think of a diagram
by a geometer with eyes of quartz.

(old dreams of a woman
half bone half diamond
with anacondas coiled against black velvet walls
and angelfish in a floor of running water!)
—and there's no choice,
you are the flute, or the music.
A cold electric trill at the moment of going
and Central Station, and the long walk
past puddles and the dim lake, obtusely reflecting
innumerable scalpels in the night.

Uncertain Sonnets

for Julie

1. (airport)

Her arms are gravelled at the undertow
of air flung across air as the monster flows
escaping air. A labyrinth, she knows,
is where all genial lies and no dreams go.
The shaggy dreambeast watches the golden leap
(a dream of Icarus caught in a dream) and still,
staring and weeping on a Cretan hill,
sucks at a dried-out marrowbone of sleep.
'Bloody well fly!'
                The styles of our defining
are words in sleep, and when the words are said
we lie in the conch of night, entwining
our double-crossing limbs on the double bed.
Toppling unbalanced in the wind I hear
your words lost in the labyrinth of my ear.

2. (the decisions)

Not to be human but an emerald
by Miro, in bluewash space; a Mantegna saint
battering firewings through the flaking paint
that holds him, as the painter stares appalled!
Those sages of Yeats' were never in collision
with the mind that bore them, with the womb's fires
that burned together them and their desires
because all caught in the same painted vision.
But we, being free, can lob the blazing shells
in the trajectories of our artist's will
whenever one of our painted selves rebels,
and blast the frescoes on Cassino's hill.
We make our choices, though they're all the same:
Cheat. Ignore the rules of the game.

3. (vernal equinox)

Polychromatic springtime's gay cadenza
fades, and the colour harpsichord is still,
then tinkles in the dark a chord of chill
deep green of Marvell, brittle green of Spenser.
The trees are green and silver in the rain,
in trees' bright traceries emerald peacocks roost,
in mirror-silver mail knights prance and joust
and motleys sing the summer in again.
This is the no-man's-land of time. The fingers
rustle across the keys. The scudding face
of the moon fades ...... but the tourney lingers
under long tides, in coral where jewelfish race
among lutes and visors, and the dumb sharks sail.
The surface flashes like a coat of mail.

4. (for George Seferis)

> Give us, beyond sleep, serenity
>
> —George Seferis

Delicate veined pale green sepals arching in nightfall's
    turquoise quiver
as the pink mullet quivers at the fishing-fork, and sway
as reeds sway in tumultuous blues, ungathering before day
falls into the same landscape: grey sea, yellow sky, glass river.
Sleep enfolded you in green leaves. Verde
que te quiero verde. And the same crows still horn the moon,
the same acanthus, oleander, flittertongue lizard, ready
in the dust at the bottom of late afternoon
to slide acid-yellow across evening, to shade eyes
glaucous against the light, to whiten and wash away
love eyesight and memory, bleach joy and blind surprise
rooting and scuttling. River and sea and sky faded to grey
yet unseen light endures; and yours was a language: for
the flood of light in the dream Samuel Palmer saw.

5. (directions for dreamfishing)

First you must blow a bottle round your sleep
in concave bottle-greens of drifting seas
around dreams' hot vermilions, where unease
will abrogate its fishing rights to deep
seas where your Dreamfish, bred and interbred
to swim upnight with what you most desire,
slides through the streaming cellstrands in your head
stippled with swirling wet St Elmo's fire
and surfacing flutters on the midnight wind,
as fish can't, as you know. The night is green
with loss. In fading dictionaries you find
'the sea-green beryl, or aquamarine.'
You wake in Billingsgate, haggling for a drab
dead slice of Dreamfish on a beryl slab.

In Memoriam

for John Forbes

A painting would have been the best way to get things over
but my father's old Winsor & Newtons still sit in their tin box
unused for three years except for when I painted
a shoddy flamboyant number on our front door.
They have hardened and cracked like introverted poets.

Coloured inks will soak through the best bond paper
in a soft fuzz of amoebas, a sunset blur
of fruit-coloured clouds, a weak ambiguous vision.
I could never use chalk or charcoal.
The poem must stalk on its own thin mantis legs.

We become, in any case, too attached to colour.
Graphite and lignite, slate and marble
that make cliff-faces, monuments, holes in the ground
have a greater permanence in their crumbling way
but aren't what we like to look at

or not in themselves. Ever since we learned about emblems
and correspondences, we have mirrored ourselves in the sea
and the rock; and the subtle shadowed faces
of our friends and rivals, as the light changes, reflect
the obliquities of our shadows, our syntax, our blood.

O'Hara, Berryman, Seferis, Pound
have a lot in common. Not only are they all dead poets
but they make up a metrically perfect line
running on iambic sleepers to whatever personal
ameliorations I think, for me, they're good for.

And that's the way the game goes. Reading the Saturday papers
and the cultured magazines, I find my nightmares visited
by a terrible vision of contemporaries writing elegies
notebooked and rainslicked at the graveside
or serial as Magritte's windows or Dunne's time

in a recession of identical rooms.
Whether there is particular grief in the deaths of poets
is a question that much engages us,
that we answer always in the affirmative,
a priori, because it's very useful to us to do so.

Pale watercolour lovers in the pastel sun
we can rape and chomp our friends' corpses at midnight,
hunch and sidle in the morgue, our eyes
a tracery of red veins in the Gothick crypt, and the tourist
maps show Transylvania's regular trains, its ordered roads.

Because it does come down to rape, this invasion
of one's substance by that of another
without connivance. And not the strongest or fiercest
can fight it, but must lie back and open
up to the slime and spawn.

Death and rebirth myths are made by poets, and no wonder:
one Dransfield can feed dozens of us for a month,
a Webb for years. And they're fair game, we can plead continuance,
no poet ever died a poet: as the salt muck filled Shelley
the empyrean gave way to the nibbling fish and the cold.

I should have hauled out the oils and tried to do a townscape
after all, a grey square with stoas and colonnades
toothed with eroding busts, their long shadows staining
each other and the foreshortened watchers'
death-watch beetle-scuttle across clattering bleached stone.

For the fan of letters opens and shuts and the wind blows
errant zig-zags of light and night through the phrases,
chops, remoulds, effaces. Theologians
have always found dismembered cannibals tough.
The whole thing becomes too tight, which is not at all

what's needed, whatever sensualists may say.
Too like Zen archery, too painful somewhere around
what used to be called the heart. The parataxis
of time and light could have flowed around and through
these dead and living poets and myself.

That would have been a pretty nonsense. Instead the flicker—
flicker of a zoetrope. In this peepshow world
all styles come down to punctuation. O Mayakovsky,
Buckmaster, all of you, they're circumventing Euclid.
They knew that parallel lines in curved space meet

eventually, somewhere: in the black hole between spaces,
the full stop with no sentence on either side,
between the moving magic-lantern slides.
Not that you wouldn't have gone there yourselves willingly:
where the blood pours out the dead come to the feast.

Microclimatology

1. Pebble

Other people have amber beads on strings
with wrought-silver clasps. Do you hear?—
you're not the only pebble on the beach,
lounging wry there among inert shells.
No work of art: neat silverpoint quarter-smile,
glissando of skin-coloured stone
curved into spring-onion head,
long Paul Klee face.
All right. A small achievement
in the palm of my hand
not quite amused.
You should be on the end of a pencil.
Pebble pregnant with the fear
that there never was a Cheshire Cat—our smiles
our wrinkles: have we been framed?
Ah, but I could tease archaeologists with you
pretending you're Cycladic
(so much younger than you are)

2. The Unreality of Roosters

I have come reluctantly to the conclusion
that sexual dimorphism is, in chickens, a fake.
Actually, by turns fluffy scrawny and stout,
they contrive continually—*in posse*
or in fact—
eggs
until, the menopause supervening
and all their creative powers quite dried up,
kindly Nature allows them
(by way of a pension)
to look finally like Governors-General.

3. Winter Solstice

I

Small chill reflections
roll around striking each other with steel clicks:
migraine marbles, blotting-paper pinball.

II

Yes, Magritte was right: clouds *are* like loaves of bread.
But what he forgot to note was the agony
of the impact, from some miles up, upon one's head
of bullet-hard seeds of celestial sesame.

III

Summer presents itself as fictive paisley
but there is something unconvincing
in the all-too-microscopic mandalas of snowdrops.

IV

The wind recapitulates the ancient
present moment
when all the duck-shaped jugs of Thera
spilled into pumice-patterned green.
It's blown the castle off the hill
and the nude poppies
were at last able to be assumed
into bronze necklaces
no one ever found, under Pelasgian walls
patched through and through
almost equally elusive rumoured sheepfolds.

V

It's little consolation to a water-ice,
when it remembers having been a man,
to be praised for delicacy of flavour.

VI

The peaks across the bay are feet deep in seagulls
and still
in fading smudges recede rapidly over the water.

VII

A sky this size coordinates
better with Riemann's view of space.
Such a curvature is unarguable
even now as it contracts, contracts
(and me inside)
—as to embracing it, however,
something less ample, less Junonian, frankly—

VIII

Defrosting and subsequent refreezing ruin the taste.
This explains both the persistence of Golden Age myths
and their continual enfeeblement.

IX

O wild west wind, I apostrophise you: notice me!
But do please be discreet about it.

X

Under white midwinter sun   the air's bleached fabric is
    stamped
with a repeating pattern of black-and-grey-striped cats and
    still-wet golden berries.

XI

The flies are still alive—
I begin to grasp Dante's penology.

XII

You have to just go
up   and then pause
a little up
there, said
Nijinsky.

And Gide said, of fish, that 'they die
belly-upward, and float
to the surface; it is
their way of falling.'

Before dawn the fishing boats
float into floating mist that certainly conceals
little prospect of a light descent
from reportable middle regions in solid air,
freeze there, hunch
back under cover, steel
sea, boats, fish, a single liquid
falling, slow horizontal rain, through the dark bedroom.

XIII

One hadn't expected—
one hardly welcomes—
the discovery of wicked Popes in the kitchen freezer.

XIV

These infinitely various mirrorings attest,
in all their shadings and elisions, perspective-shifts,
outrush and inflow of colour, cathexes of light,
the singular unacknowledged virtues of never washing
    the window.

XV

The streets will run green and scarlet with molten birdsong,
perhaps, in spring

4. The Evidence

It isn't as though there'd been no warning.
The clues were literally everywhere, we kept stumbling
over the evidence; really, the ploys
of misdirection should have been all too apparent.
Why, for instance, did that triple rainbow
salt its tail in urchin-speckled offshore
searocks, for a sly moment, and then snap back
into church like a guerilla hatband? The Minoan bowl
of translucent rose-glass, figured with cloudy octopi and squid,
who clapped it down on top of the White Mountains
and snipped off the curls of seaweed, the parched
articulations of foothill cactus and thyme?
Where did they come from, those T'ang illuminati-in-exile
with their scrolls and inkpots? Rain indeed.
And the flag of bees? The snow in the roofed market
scribbling sententiae all over the melons?
—I need hardly mention the shotguns cycling tandem up
    the ravine,
the goats that kept dropping out of fig trees,
the grandmother who turned into a sickle.
But there's no use denying it,
by the time the wind danced off with the breakwater
we'd all been completely taken in. And even now,
look, again everyone is gathered, staring and pointing.
O the ineptitude!—Somewhere else a quite unpeopled miracle
    occurs.

5. The Rent

It has been less than satisfactory.
The chickens, fortunately, are too much chickens
to remember how yesterday I nearly brained them,
as they fuddled around in the garbage pit,
with a half-gallon retsina bottle.
If those chickens did catch on
I wouldn't give much for our chances.

And when I suddenly found myself
heaving, among other things, into that same pit
a florid authoritative rat—
when the landlord's small daughter tottered in
with a wilted radish,
wanting, I knew from experience,
to operate in exchange upon the typewriter—
when the landlord threatened to cut our friend's feet off—

and so we left, giving them
little gilt Qantas kangaroos.

6. The House

for Nadia

There is no need to talk about the light.
The solid mountains blow about the gate,
young cats and yellow frogs in the rosemary
are still, meticulous. (Our tree
promised mulberries, but three weeks late.)
An owl nearby ticks night.

We've climbed very slowly up the hill
where the asphodel flower like quotations
from a poem we never quite understood.
The beach was crosshatched with driftwood,
stippled with reeds. There are other creations
round us; first drafts of spiders on the sill.

In this bay within a bay times drift through the pines:
the watering-lady in the garden floats
breaststroke out of lumps of marble or walls
frescoed under whitewash. When the owl calls
she vanishes, leaving stout black petticoats
nodding over the roses, pruning vines.

7. Notes from the Noctarium

I

Hedgehog,
your coiffure
repels all contumely. Why then are you yourself
thus transparent-soft, mousevelvet
quivering on my coat? You rely on trust?
Come now,
surely your hairdresser could recommend also
a health studio?

II

When they cut down the plane trees in the square
the owl moved into one of our pines.
But small elegant bodgie birds come and wake him up
and josh him in blank daylight. Ah where now is the old club,
worn armchair and definite cigar
far above the traffic,
light pouring down the wet black streets?

III

The frogs still hop, awkward and if they've time,
into weed-patches, building-lots and bathrooms.
Our houses are built on gauzy traceries
of silhouetted frogs. You can scan them,
comic strips,
as they sink gradually into what we call asphalt.
The frog prince married a tractor wheel;
their fairy tale is altogether different.

8. The Benefactors: Mr. Achillopoulos' Mercantile School (Mt Pelion, Thessaly)

Suddenly the bus whizzed onto the sliding glaze
of perhaps the last surviving green-figure amphora
(traditional centaur workmanship) of the lost school of Pelion.
Needlepointed with a pox of fog-pits
or vindictively pricked by dead demented lapiths, patterned
with the unmistakable knotting of plane
and horse-chestnut trees, figure
on ground of wet slate and shale. Horsehair in pores of
    sooty marble,
arrow-poison veining the forest floor.

'... the wrong discipline ... disciplined ...
A stork booms in the high wind.
"Have mercy, Lord, for we have sinned."'

The plane
tree, good for hanging a dozen bishops, encircled
by seven wooden benches void
of their old men, sweeps shale (now brown with coffee-grounds
and wild-mulberry juice) paving the chill
silent village square, and mossfur on slate roofing
the dissolved cottages of woodcutters
down in the horse-chestnuts where the village hides.

Brambles and roses clog the door
and vacant niche intended for
the statue of the Governor.

All the old men were
forked into the cobbles they'd crammed upright
for mules' grip (still the hooves like running children
suddenly lost in a green stick-insect, and timber
or cocoons cascading) entering
an altogether new taxonomy. From grey-green fretworks of sky
the plane tree fountains down in
five-fingered leaves.

Chinks in the shale are round with rain.
The old men visit once again
the church at the end of Donkeyshit Lane.

But squeeze under the portcullis of white roses
that spill from eyeholes in the grass-snakes'
and cornflowers' habitat, and skip the stinging nettles
and the illusive niche between mirror staircases
receding to a horizon in the pineal eye, scratch on
slate.
Where the blackboards have all fallen through the rotten floor
nouns in the ossuary-chapel, verbs
trapped in plane leaves. The process:

Candlewax and lamp-oil spatters.
Priests mutter, the cantor chatters.
They will all rise as mad as hatters.

Mr Socrates Achillopoulos, the Benefactor,
parsed into landscape circa 1909, finds himself compounding
syntactical trunk-murders down every damp trail,
the topology police hot after his flow.
Everywhere springs labelled Undrinkable, or clotted
with a fat paste of leaves (under a tap
a black-and-yellow ladybird swims in a tin can
like a tiny galley after a lost battle.)

—the ceiling drips a pool of staph
the temperature's shot off the graph
there's gangrene sauce on the pilaf—

Claustrophobia on the outside of a vase? Nonsense,
cheap tricks of perspective and inversion, words
that can't be faced unless they're vases
or fishtanks or frescoes—and after all
they're so easy. 'It's only nerves.'
Earthenware, splotched with fake primaries
or strewn with twilight differentials of green on green,
walls, it doesn't matter. The lie's a continuity of trees
without reference to the footsteps receding
into leaves, into paint ......

Outside, three kittens chasing a gecko leap
onto the jumbled ancestors, asleep
in their tin boxes, scrabble in the heap

of promises dug into wood and stone
each assuring to each alone
transfiguration in the bone.

Long ago the notorious geometry toxin
stretched their lives into a pattern of such surfaces
as jugs, pots, a village-square and a sun
green as breakers, a transformational
grammar of horse-chestnuts. The naming of parts:
dactylic plane leaves, 'Old Handy' 'dead
of weddings', church wall and green vase,
all the dismal perquisites of love.

Chestnut leaves block the dry spout.
The kittens tumble the tins about.
Slate and sky shut evening out.

Cheiron and Mr Achillopoulos are equally
scattered. Incredible. And we saw in a flash
—it seemed so simply apprehensible—
hidden tilted villages with no sky but plane leaves
falling away over the curve of the world
past woods and belltowers. Poured
with the shake of a hand into another sphere
of knife-edge cobbles and jammed taps; falling
at last forever away from the sun.

Leviathan looms out of the narthex wall.
The whore straddles her beast. Worms crawl
over the blackening damp. Souls fall and fall.

Cyclops Songs

1. Esprit De L'Escalier

Good manners, sir, are an infernal machine,
and unjuicing your companions a problem in tact
'at the meeting of two value-systems.' If
you complain, so may I. Sir, I am an ogre
not a structural linguist. Even so I understood,
of course, your ridiculous alias, and I knew
perfectly well what 'Noman is hurting me' meant,
but I played by the rules. So now my face feels like
    pork-crackling,
looks like it too, I imagine. You've ruled yourself out,
made yourself Noman indeed. But how would you have done
on *my* IQ tests? Did you get my jokes?
Next time around we'll understand each other,
next time I'll ask you round the back.
I, for one, am going to make sure I get it right.

2. The Afterimage

Always the ship's echo drifts over
my eyelid's charred puckered rag. Always yellow,
the daisies exploding—the meadow beyond the laurel tangle—
the remembered pitch hull, the vermilion cheeks, are gone:
like the blind librarian I wear a yellow filter, and it may say
something about anger that yellow won't go away,
about injustice: singing out *my* rage
—'ignorant of all laws and of good custom'—I sing
for my flock and the village nymphets
who screech and scamper off when they peek over the byre wall
and see the singer—when raving Achilles
can strut through the agapanthi like a bronze walking-fish
and I stew in the broth of unsavoury songs.
All night the ship comes and goes, comes and goes, moors
    just out of reach.

3. Goya's 'Colossus'

If my verses seem conventional
this is because I live inside a pastoral
convention. I break it up
every morning when I clump down to the beach, a ram in
    each hand
for good companionship, practising Braille,
studying the cave-bats' knack of radar. Nor am I
Emily Post. I squat enormous at the edge of things
and breathe heavily, Gnarrh, at the frightened villages. Yet
the flock trails tapestries of brass bells, the ship
in my head bucks, elegant and sleepy, against
my long-suffering skull, and I skim ducks-and-drakes
across the numb inlet.
                      It makes itself whole again; I'm sewn
again, each coolly synthesised evening,
rocks flocks and all, into my seamless formal chrysalis.

4. The Homecoming

Well, what *was* Odysseus good at? (1) making things (2) lying—
neither a skill I've any use for. Don't talk to me
about subtlety. I've travelled too,
smelt caique-decks' tar and goat and onions in milky dawn winds,
snoozed hunched in my fur on offal wharves, and remember
prayer-flagged cairns, moon-priestesses and pig-myths
on steppes beyond the writ of American Express.
And come back betraying nobody—Argo, Argus,
I'm my own device and my own dog: 'Beware the Savage Cyclops.'
Why should *I* lie?
                      But for instance I miss
the lobster-scamper down seaweed-stinking alleys,
away from fearful demonstrations yelling
Support Your Local Triple Goddess.—To bed—
I'll give you 'sodden toward sundown'.

5. Some Versions of Pastoral

He ate my cheese; he tried to steal my sheep.
And I'm too huge and ugly and male to be a poltergeist
and big rocks are easily to hand, so I squash things.
What's it to me if my brothers built Tiryns?
                                        Uncle Toms.
I have my flocks and overgrown laurel and no intention
of handing either over, or making them out
to be more than they are. The laurel's for hiding
and sure enough Nymphs and Shepherds do just that
so I bawl my love song and stamp on them too;
they asked for it. My eye was round as a cartwheel
with amazement: I wondered about things
and was happy when they wondered back,
I staked myself on reciprocity. But now
'I want to be alone'; why not from me?

6. The Recidivist

But just consider his subsequent career.
Eight years of gluey fucking, interspersed
with the occasional peeved Please miss I wanna go home.
Then the bullyboy muscleman act—gunning down
every younger better-looking bloke for miles around—'O man
of many devices!'—Killa Godzilla, more like it.
And a kink about bondage.
                            The thrushes flutter in the greased noose.
And then after all that the stickybeak gods
had to be flown in from Athens or wherever
like a mob of arbitration commissioners. You:
I'm talking about you. But at least,
you bastard, blind as I am, and a hostage
to your stiff-twined cordon of darkness, *I*
am still the one who writes the poems.

The Typewriter, Considered as a Bee-Trap,

is no doubt less than perfectly adapted
to its function, just as a bee-trap,
if there are such things, would hardly be the ideal contrivance
for the writing of semi-aleatory poems about
bee-traps and typewriters. Why, in any case,
you are entitled to ask, should I
want to trap bees at all? What do with them
if caught? But there are times, like today,
when bees hover about the typewriter
more frequently than poems, surely knowing best
what best attracts them. And certainly at such times,
considered in terms of function and structure,
the contraption could be argued to be
anything but a typewriter,
the term 'anything' being considered
as including, among all else, bee-traps,
softly multiplying in an ideal world.

Aristarchus and the Whale

Let us, to pass the time as we cycle
to where we'll fish, retell
the old, old tale we used to love hearing
at bedtime or in Sunday-school
of how, persecuted by the tyrant Polycrates
for building bicycles without a licence,
Aristarchus of Samos, on the advice
of his old tutor Pythagoras (now something
high up in the corridors of power),
took refuge in the great fish
until, centuries later, it was caught
by several fishermen simultaneously
(another story, that)
to the immense and justified alarm
of Polycrates, who had read
in an old almanac (he was, poor fellow,
superstitious) that should something of the sort
occur, he was in for
a nasty end, and had consequently adopted
the alias of 'Urban VIII' (and wore for protection
a signet-ring stamped with a fish),
none of which helped him, bicycles
emerging from the whale's maw in endless implacable streams
having rolled over and over him ever since,

while Aristarchus' subsidiaries,
under a variety of names,
have taken out floods of patents
on up-to-date systems of gears;
let us by all means retell the old tale
even if, when younger, we may have
misinterpreted the moral. Ah,
but the one that got away!

Annula

Here everyone lives around holes:
bells in a bell-shaped mosque,
a trench full of fat white turkeys roosting in fig-trees,
bullet holes in the window. Runnels ellipse
fingernail slivers of spray, gales ring under the doorjamb.
Saucers of sunflower seeds dot the café motif, fall
into a landscape poem, favourite genre
of their and our favourite century. A poem of small landscapes;
last page bottom column-inch of the local paper
(our elections, yes) spilling across the racked
endless spaces of exile from a particular moment.
The sodden awning plays
two scratched prints of not quite the same movie
charring, curling despite the floating harbour,
strung between the pole we set off from and the one
we don't yet seem to have arrived at, although it's here,
surrounding us, as we arrange patterns of seeds in a spill
    of paper.
Later we line up the husks in armies.
Five centuries the seawall
and still combers lollop over the tables
where they still wait for the Turks.

The cannon are sunken into bollards, but the expected contrast
elusive—always, to be sure,
just this unreadiness, just this repetition: we can't take a tough line,
only the illusion that here we include history, and look
for history through empty windows
behind palm fronds and Blue Peters, focus
on ancient idiot blue, the slew of bikes
and slap of boots on the slipways, the northern breakers
over the galleys' moorings. Nothing but skinny cats
fishing in seaweed; the connections are cut.

These ductile scraps of guidebook time: the film-clips flicker
out of synch, the filter in the window
tessellates in splashes of light, random,
any old colour: shuffle against the night.

To the Innate Island

for Grace Edwards and in memory of
Katina Androulidaki and Nikos Papasifakis

Astros—Athens—Mystra—Monemvasia—Yannina—Metsovo—Chania—
Phaistos—Kastoria—Thessaloniki—London—Sydney, 1977–1980

1. The Shadow Screen

The small grey cat in the yard has a knack for the punctuational.
Confronted with unfamiliar yoghurt, it curls
bristling into a fluid query, later ingratiates
itself into tactful receding aposiopesis towards the garbage-bag,
illuminated exclamation over the yellow light
of a butterfly to be slapped and broken, lays out evenings
in commas at the window, sentences from Proust
lapping to night where all cats are grey.

Spreads its net of signs, assumes
the harbour and the lights folded into the hills, and we see
suddenly from within the cat's eye; itself
or a merely perceiving Maxwell's demon, see eye and world
and shifting waterline between them, uneasy
that over the sea fauve stripes flow, our old paintings
of a felt jungle pulling back
the keen small mind of a cat, retracting its claws
temporary, promissory, conditional
upon a saucer of milk—yet do they see colours at all?

'Caught while attempting escape':
                              a tinge of sun
slid away past a lost flash of thought, apt cat's eye,
fastened onto the suggestion of a web
of just such salmon-silver scales as just then the harbour
flaunting when the white daze of streetlamps snapped along
    the mole
dropped into place to the acetylene
fishing-boats' drumbeat in a slick of rain
scattered over the twisting blue scarf of the beach.

2. Finding Islands

> Springwater grow so thick it gonna clot
> and the pleasing ladies cease. I figure, yup,
> you is bad powers.
>
> —John Berryman

We walked among coelenterate rocks, fossils of water.
'Everything grew old in a single night', parching
in the white centipede stretched between us and the sun.
Scattered concrete poems
fingerprints are distilled from whirlpools
creation myths
typed one-fingered by a desk-sergeant.
A night's miscegenation of basalt and orchids,
'Foetus', 'hawthorn-blossom', plugging the cracks
of patient years' alembicated
clotted engraving; mad monks' days under these mountains.
The island in the lake
scatters itself just below the surface in sherds and ash,
the trout feed on seventeen dear dead ladies.

The sky was thick with hermits on eagleback,
Tiepolo thrones in the verdigris mist, pale blue and gold; far below
an ochre scarab crawled through the clouds' carillon,
Theofanis of Crete, ragged and barefoot, with his paintbox
and bag of figs, trudging to the island through the peacock's tail.

Wedged at the foot of a rooftop ladder of roosters,
fed up at last with the tyrants of his fancy,
concrete high-rise of his texts erasing the green-white
marble sun into cave-lime, with principles
Meno's lads heresiarchs and Dionysus,
Plato gone white thinks that he dreams of the island,
    dreams that he knows
where to find it, knows he's long boasted of knowing
the long lie of how to get there
                                    (while new-moon bindlestiffs,
fringed and striped, drift up through Wallachia,
Moldavia, hill-villages of smoke and dung, into worlds of grass,
over snow and lava, paying out
the luminous eel of lies, shining over the horizons
from Mani to Vladivostok, littering the hoarfrost
with lives of saints, fiddlesticks and fake-amber worry beads;
'they move on dark nights in long lines'; 'only
antinomian, not free'.)
                                    At sunset the tangerine chairs
paint the electroplating on the tape-recorder.

3. The Ikonostasis

The dark years are signed with a break in the ribbons of stone
where the hammers were lost in the reeds, where toads eels
    leeches
work out a rapprochement, nibbling away at the island:
it takes minutes less to walk round: draining the lake:
the abbot skis down on pentecost with mayfly-wings
    of dead monks
and calcined owls: to the swamp
where only yesterday the lake was.

There are niches to crawl into, cave-systems to explore, lakes
under the lake. The butterfly floor-boards cluster round the light
rippling with midges and mosquitoes. Behind the curtain
the caverns are said to be crammed
with statues of philosophers and their famous faithful dogs.

The blue gloom offers a lacquered screen, walnut and
    pear-wood: here
an orphan girl pierced on a sickle of sunlight
traces the pictograph calendar's glossy bright tin-label
    day-saints, and here
a nun slides across whitewash by candlelight, here
a cat shadow-boxes a pot of geraniums.
Slow moon-burnished fish carry the island away on their
    backs into night.

A brocaded doll pouts in the corner, staring
and pointing anywhere but at the secret passage
from the crypt to the pulsing air-bubble where we live.
Four small elephants skid on a tortoise's back
and the monasteries slide down the hill, into the water.
Bow to your partner.

4. Cross In The Water

Epiphany comes in a clicking display-case of insectine frost.
   Only in Wu Ch'eng-en
perhaps, and even then
only when Kuan-yin's caught, or the Jade Emperor, on a good day,
do the airy bureaucrats arrange
these silverblue feather skies, high cyclamen triremes, balloons
floating out into cold till there's no more space and the sun's gone,
while lazy sea-dragons tumble just underwater
(as a sheet's ripple-pattern susurrus shapes unseen sleepers)
and the Gorgon never asks after Iskander
and the priest fails to fall in the sea.

As for me
with my beaten-up Book of Songs, repository
of unvisitable yellow-paper puppets, umbrella
for grateful errors,
there are still to be heard under the birds in the puffs of mimosa
Milinda's questions, the answers of Nagasena.
If we can cobble this—
if somewhere there's an oliveleaf-soapstone Buddha with
   a Greek face
then in lakebottom silt there will splash the ambiguous cross
inscribed: 'Aristu,
Aflatun.' We can transit, take up possession and go
taking with us this tiny and silted-up harbour, this slow
aggregate too of subtractions of things to define it—
they still call it 'The Island'—
make trelliswork, beanpoles and pine-branches
to hold up the screen of water where simple bright-coloured
   creatures
without homes or dimensions will strut us their dance
under cinnamon sun

and a fizzy moon, green
and delusive as spearmint chartreuse, or the weeds that plaited
 their hair

in the land of postcards. Green rotting heads there
devolve back to scum, and the strings of blue beads
round their necks crawl off under crayfish—
there's a plot if you think there is—
always read between the lines.
The fact is connections are free, though sometimes
there are carkers in corners, thieves demand toll as you pass
 through the mountains,
odd polite strangers inquire after presents
or a note comes from Dr Moreau: 'Draw the curtains.
There's one devil too many.' People rush out and the show ends.

5. The Monemvasia Causeway

On Malmsey rock the nerves converge,
wintry throb of veins,
tortoise pulsing asleep in still water.
The red thread of granny's autobahn
moving south down the bloodstream
unfolds genetic codes of guards
of this rock (this empire)—grumbling at knucklebones,
gulping hot barley beer, boiling
sheepsheads in cauldrons of Greek fire.
At six in the morning
cocooned in wind
we catch the Sparta bus.
Stench of invisible goatskin jerkins,
worn leather corselets eyeleted with frayed string—
they drowned in the twisting archways' shark's jaw,
seas of sheet-lightning, rain and bells,
waiting for the crescent to burst over the blotch of mountain.
The rock's folded into churches,
ironstone owls peck at the prickly-pear.
Castles hammered into the rock
slid away with the rock,
windows filled with broken glass,
the gate's sheath rusted before our eyes;
horned helmets over the causeway.
The sea made sounds of sleep
and we slipped from our posts at the high wall
past thistle pastures where goats played
to the weedy plates shifting under the island,
we saw the pirates arrived at last
without bullion or black eyepatches
with faces like our own in the tarnished mirror's
jonquil-crowned hyacinth-spattered stone.

6. Friezes

> These were the 'Wing'd-with-Awe',
> Inviolable...
>
> —Ezra Pound

Most of the Titans thought a plenum best
but were slow thinkers, earthed: never looked back
to see how, as they crammed the sky
in pursuit of an ideal, pits yawned
where Ossa and Pelion had stood.
Just one flashed across like the bird that ate him,
the rest were all smeared
into that lowlanders' invention, landscape.
Then first things could at last be first
and there were solitudes to die in
to songs repeating from cassettes in fugue.

Round they go, dancing with clumsy steps, round,
the slow labouring figures, always in profile, never
speaking, or touching, each bone-heavy
with sense of unbearable self, chained down with
integrity, marching away off the frieze
to reappear, we know, at a fixed time
forever, after just as awkwardly
negotiating the other side. Look
at the size of their feet. There's no question
of being afraid. Compact of gravity they'll walk right through you
and no one the wiser
from the ripple of transient lightness.

Another image is of an avenue
gridded with lime trees, and a flow
of stately girls with hoops,
barberpole-striped football players in green stasis
and glossy feathered soldiers eating ice-cream.
Painters in navy-blue berets sketch prams and oranges,
the first leaves have always just fallen.
That is another place. But even so,
in a third picture, looking-glasses show
memory-places out of Paul Delvaux.
One of the girls, now shown
under the petticoats to be made of beeswax,
stands alone at the foot of the staircase
sputtering with a small flame. Outside it snows.

The first one issues from behind a screen,
or through a green baize door, or the cold fireplace.
The sculpted mud snakes round his ears.
He doesn't look back. (Cuneiforms of bird-tracks
wiped out under the huge silent dance.)
Eventually they will all have passed through the room
again. Now nothing moves.
The trees have become streetlamps
with orange grins. The wind moves under the snow.

In marble cafeteria corridors
the *kouroi* strut and preen
twiddling their tinplate keychains
and all around them flicker the quick blue sparks of neurosis.
Ah, close your eyes, play the guitar.
The knobbed mountains are bleak as alfoil, and the dance
only the unsquarable signature
on the document that proves us many.

7. From the Folk-Song Archives

> Repression, however, is not the most obvious characteristic
> of the sea.
>
> —Marianne Moore

Two by two, the Founders carry their monasteries between them
like large delicate cakes.
That's the good part. Prefer
penny plain to tuppeny coloured, try to see
through the cat's eye, or (must be) translated Proust,
tracing the music. The tape-recorder
weaves its cobweb map. Across the portolan, songs drift
north, in the stained lint-filled pockets
of wandering iconographers-turned-cantor.
The mountain-spines are strung on the swaying notes
of secular songs vintaged out under white kid knee-boots.
The landscape balloons,
rises to hills high
enough to fall from, lakes
deep as drowning.
After the shadow-play we do the real thing.

Amours de voyage: scaled seas flow
in the pour of dawn to the Cretan mountains,
Hercules' Pillars, those Odysseus saw last.
Flecks of colour emerge, scatter of flags out of night.
An exercise in ethnomusicology: Marsyas' flute,
Hope's kastura, the women of Zalongo,
Mirbeau's bell, bells banged
with rumoured Belgian priests, the possibilities
the Flemish masters found in harps; small spotted dogs

cocking an ear at the Iron Maiden.
The dead-bell splintered the whole morning.
We don't look closely at the saints' faces
in the scraps of fresco when the sirens sound.
Cracked modern windows rattle in the dome's bare brick;
the Pantokrator's not at home.

8. The Bills

The air has been thick with typescripts of imaginary
    conversations. For instance,
having paid just the first of an irrational number of bills
we sat smiling at each other like fools, and at the salad of cabbage
ribbed with intractable thick central veins, the tepid spaghetti
and wine buzz-bombed by tiny precocious flies, hard by
    the beach,
discussing not bills but butterflies. One, beachcombing,
settled near our table, lemon-yellow spotted with burnt orange.
You asked, and I don't know, about the ones that kill mice
    and small birds:
they're surely too light, we agreed, too weak, whatever their
    wingspan,
can hardly have fangs, constrictor coils, glands full of poison?
(At this point a gull zoomed across our heads and presented
a preschool crayon of itself out over the bay.)
But what was to become then of Chuang Tzu's dream?
Silently we may have concluded that figure and carpet
had been switched on us, tried
to preserve the morning's occasions from infection. No doubt,
after all, those butterfly-tigers
in fact pay their bills meekly enough, their coshes and
    derringers stashed
safely away back home; all deference
to a black-beetle with a deal desk. And the gull is a hole in the sky?
One candlestick, then, or two profiles?
Not 'or', perhaps: 'and'. Thought to have hit on the trick
of the moment when penicillin flies in the window
like the angel of the annunciation, or Kepler's wrong sums
cancel each other out. 'For God's sake,' someone said,
'give that spider back to Robert Frost.'

'What spider?'—but he always has the last word and fades back into my own answer. The spider that trapezed in between the lines, disguised as a startling new synthesis about butterflies.

9. A Drink at the Exploding Monastery

How you awake now you awake if you awake at all
is your own business, but a friendly warning:
the clay water pitcher's lying on its side
in the far corner, a faint smell of damp dust at the bottom;
a dry lemon-leaf will fall out when you pour,
olive-pips, a handful of chickpeas; cornucopia.
You filled it only last night, you'll say, and slept
while any number of moons rose and set,
unfamiliar stars bobbed across a greased sky
while smoke-clouds billowed from the pine groves. Really—
and sighting back, long silver-chased gun for a lever,
you shoved aside world after world through tunnels
    of small waves
at fish-eye level: or grew groined windows
cloisters and bell-towers and suddenly blew up
(in the dream a charred child was found in a copse nearby
and lived to lie about it many years after)
and round you rows of crones picked wild spinach
dandelion greens cardoon, cracking their nails
on the scorched rock where the red mill-stream ran.
And despite yourself you'll dream
of when there were wild ibex up past the high forests,
when there were the forests themselves,
when the brigantines came in with black wine
and the sea-caves were stuffed with hardtack and gunpowder.
By all means suck on leaves. The jar's
just large enough now to creep into. Remember
red cells live on long after the man they lived in
survivors too feeble to loot the abandoned city
dull-burning sphere of sunset.

10. Psychopannychy

'Thinking about it only makes it worse.' Raises a brow, a plateau,
and as more think more stretches it to stocking-mask tautness,
no longer quivering, altogether quiet. Now
it's all cracked bone-dry lake-floor, hot brown, ridged
with scratched-in cobwebs, scrapings, negative wickerwork
where reeds were, fingerbones, quill pens.
Fists and feet pass through you,
pellets of dried mud rattle against your eyes, straggler,
rise and shine; the sun's been up for days.
All the sky's here, begged borrowed stolen,
since oxygen's first faint bow, and from every
enamel-azure altar-screen or ikon since say St Luke:
figure-eight shield's weight of the first yawning
feeling, vision when the alarm clock rings.
And under all the skies are all the men.
Now it's no good referring back to Daumier's
thing coming up through the trapdoor, Redon Piranesi Munch,
things you insisted were nightmares,
the Premature Burial, the Pit.
'I don't dream: never had a dream in my life.'
Good. Now you're on the neutron star,
the leaden bedclothes no less than what you are. Yet you're
    surrounded
on all sides by all that's brittle, breakable:
egg-shells and the skulls of birds, clocks, kites,
rosewood clavichords, bamboo flutes, biplanes,
paper flowers, glass shrimps.

All the horizons shone with the twelve gilt numbers,
the rings endless, no matter that you dig deeper,
the heaviness comes also from below. Look
at the growth-rings in the petrified forest, and the perfect colour
you stupidly thought just brown. You've seen it before,
that particular luminous baby blue, on murals
hot on the right with gold as you looked out,
red to the left, dropping through fishmouths.
(There were panics, rumours
that some angels had been caught shaving the weights,
that every 'night'
deserters tiptoed out through the ashen campfires.)
Now, as we crawl through the screens, sleep's over. Now
    the specific
after we'd all caught clocks so badly. We make up
hundreds of words for different edible grasses,
kinds of snow, soft drinks, cars.
What did I tell you about REM sleep? But don't worry,
the electrodes have vanished like the grass.
Open your eyes again: you see, they've put in new lenses.
'Dreams are no substitute
for the decision-making process.'

11. Water-Garden Snapshots

In the inner garden which we never visit
the insects proceed quietly
about their unlearned webwork of small occasions,
the cat a cloud behind the bay-branches,
and the boat moves into the bay.
In a syringe,
we travel among islands,
are fire-hardened splinters, toxin-tipped, in Atlantis.
The hedgehog snoozes under a bush,
lizards bask on the wall, the cat
floats lower, rain at the edges of its eyes.
The boat slides in, grazes on the pebbles, retracts.
The cat withdraws behind the bay-tree,
inspects the chinks in the wall, the scattered berries
and oh-so-casually retiring lizards, and on the horizon
the boat seems to be coming in, rust-red sail
onset of a study in pointillism, still
all promises; the cat rolls on the sun-blank doorstep.

Or think of the moment
most poignant in the
process of
parting
suggested by a water-drop's
almost less than momentary
moment's defiance
of gravity, the point
at which its top goes
convex, as it splits
off from what is becoming the next drop.

Or land at last and view the conventional scene:
oil-slicks and oil-logged gulls, fist-sized lumps of tar,
aerosols, beer-cans and blue plastic bags. And mosquitoes,
midges, caddis larvae, fat spiders, culture and nature.
This is the point where the script indicates: *acceptance*:
do you like it? do you row off
with your cracked oars and unstopped bunghole? do you
    look back?
           The palaces have been swallowed: do you regret them?
The statues looted: will you put up new ones?
You never return to the place you started from.
Since then earth's moved, and sun, and you find
blank untwinkling stars, blood bursting through the head.
The boat's coming in, look,
that must be it, that blob rounding the cape: you cry
'Lemurs in the leaves! Is this a joke?
This is Madagascar!', and the boat fades back
in rewinding spools of ocean, and the cat takes its mask off.
Re-run, chirring in the grass,
a poppy falls, the sun sighs and enters again stage left,
old trouper, and far away are statues of small gods
with enormous baby-blue eyes. The wind blows down from
    the dunes.
The boat is loaded
with a second-hand phrenological head,
a smuggled ikon of the Last Judgment,
an insufficient supply of hardtack,
a postcard of the Disc of Phaistos, gold on blue.
In the inner garden which we never visit
the boat seems to be coming in, rust-red sail,
the cat a cloud behind the bay-branches.

12. The Whistlers of Phaistos

> Generally speaking the Villa and the whole complex of Aghia Triada has the following characteristic: it has all the things lacking from the Palace of Phaistos. That is, the Palace of Phaistos has some peculiar lacks ...
>
> —J.M. Christoforakis,
> *Crete: A Complete Traveller's Guide*

It lacks Sir Arthur Evans' red-ochre signature,
crocus-accented, visible like the snakes of Nazca
only from the sky, at Knossos: yes, and the Great Wall of China
is a get-well card to Mars. Here
the Disc dropped through the collapsing floor
into time, where we think we look at it
through glass in the museum—but opaque
and impermanent as a carbon-column, lost
the key, the scales, the music.
Perhaps it's a model of the Great Spiral Nebula,
perhaps it's a trap.
The printed glyphs curl in to the centre:
fish, scaled helmet, mailed courier
spinning down the black hole.

They perch on the pebble wall above the Plain of Messara,
three of them, an old man,
a young man, a brown wooden woman in black,
playing badly on tin-whistles to the lizards and tamarisks.
I thought later of the Inca quena,
sometimes made from the femurs of jaguars or of men.

       Round a corner
blue steel cone of silence over the terrace,
hardly a memory of footsteps, of bare feet
painted with red and gold, with blue flowers and dolphins.
Blue cupful of stones,
matchstick tree scroll; aphids weighting the carob.
Blue air's rolled over the mountain
from Lassithi plateau by five thousand windmills, across
Phaistos, the seabuilt city, without astrolabes
but star-taker itself, weaving them through leaves, pollen.

A palace at least: as unmistakably
as a couple of knucklebones and a scrap of mummy-tendon
were a diplodocus or a Father of the Church.
(There's too much missing.) Stone smile,
new peal of laughter in the rock. Zeus
the stone
moved down through the forests from Diktys
from the cobweb cave down the snake-shaped way
(Quetzalcoatl? Pizarro?) as the flutes played.
That's there: the gods walked in sharp lines of steel
and the cup cracks, everything dipped in a solution
of bluewash blue, laid out to dry on the rocks.

Circa seventeen hundred rain stopped play,
grey rain from Santorini, red rain from Argos,
gilded bullhorns wrenched the red soil away.
Grey mullet swim downbay unaware of botargo.
(The bleached snakes squirm in their tunnels,
innocent mouths hanging open, expecting milk.
There's none on the Disc; it flew
in one soundless explosion
  straight into a creation myth one invents at leisure.)
All that was left was lists, despite the professor
who read in the tablets love-lyrics in Basque.

The quipu says nothing without a remembrancer,
I can't float a poem
to South America on a papyrus boat,
can't tune the two transistors,
tin-whistle and bone flute into a chord.

Feather-crowned Snake slips through the vines,
weaves back into the floorless forest,
fades into the sleek flicker of a strobe.
The palace behaves
sometimes like particles, sometimes like waves. They step
down from the blue arches, out
from tentative gestures of surf, up
from blue mist in caves or cisterns.
The lady of the beasts takes a rain check. The three
poke at souls, scraps of paper.
She dissolves in a wave of neutrino confetti, flooding us
as we flood palace and plain.
A twittering of flutes on the transparent hill:
the palace is pulled away for the split-second
when we can't help
blinking—
by some particular last attachment, the call of a priest,
a bough breaking, sandal-strap
aflap on smooth paving-stone,
eye that sees the whole of it through time:
adjustment: and we see only
blind inner skin of our eyelids
and for so short a time we can't draw the irrational inference
to think it to a world, rightly.
The ceremony. Bunting and bands
and three tin-whistles. The elect
passed through the gates: through time and words:
spinning, onto the Disc.

Windows

It won't do, referring this spring day
back to Giotto's circle.
It whirls apart, slings off
a spinning web of swallows.
Black-and-white kittens with blue wool
they toss the May sky away.
It won't do, metaphors
whose terms are too close together.
But we walk for a moment
under the blue monkeys in the grove, and the prince of lilies.
The swallows play high-cockalorum in the eaves.
Anthropomorphism won't do.
Another day. At first
hangs in blazing waves of cloud over our heads,
bursts in accidie, numb blank shell
saying, like dreams, nothing. Another:
solar corona, genesis:
wet orange sheet hanging on the line.

It won't do, it won't do: but it does.

Reading Moby-Dick Backwards

Blake's guinea's forged: the sun's Quito doubloon
clouds over and fades to just another moon.
Lost paper sailboats float just out of reach.
I pick my way on a shredded-paper beach.
Somewhere behind the paleness, out of sight,
someone is sucking the colours from the sea,
subtracting from the world (except for me)
the strong blue smear swimming upward through the white.
A milky tsunami, moon-high, nightmare-slow,
dumps bleached scrimshanker mannikins at my feet,
half holds them back. Until it lets them go
I can't tell them from it. It won't retreat.
Peevish I poke the emerging sherds and dregs
and thump the white sea with pale dead ivory legs.

The Secret War

No one makes slide rules any more.
Through the fold on the shore, under the candystriped cycads,
    moving
out of the mainstream, earlybird
eryops, third eye acock,
slumps upmudbank, swimming-bladder itching like crazy,
    radar skew-whiff;
hears flapping. So the intelligence reports
blew it: they, the real thing, the birds
who had always been just weather, have got here first.
Say the birds: Let's bomb them back into the stone age.
His bonebound hill of head booms under the salvoes
of bullying uncomplicated beaks. They sneer at him,
their rich uncles have bought all of them twenty-speed
    racing bikes.
He bows his head and counts and counts on his odd
    webbed fingers.
Birds pick like the divine clockwork at dragonflies' twig-scroll
    tissues of gold wire.

Bonsai

All day at the flower show, 'valuing idea less for their truth than
their aesthetic content', the accredited frisson
of an all-night Tom & Jerry marathon, the wise men relax
    under the dwarf juniper
watching Chelsea Pensioners being happy-snapped drinking tea.
The structure of narrative drags the day toward Friday,
    the picknicking sages
to the snapping of bonds, wormed frail hawsers, when the wonder
in grains of sand palls as it's taken in yet again. Now they need
the bright colours, but one quotes: 'A rainbow is a colour caustic
modelled by the trivial fold catastrophe.' Rounding the cusp
the brontosaurs gallop at the Flower Arrangement Marquee
at a sprightly 2 mph. 'Have you noticed,' asks another,
    'how in a writer
it's always regarded as the final proof of greatness
when he says he keeps repeating himself?' No one can find
    the brass band.
The Americans click: 'Ready steady go. Thank you for this
    truly wonderful show.'

Bolas

> You can't step into the same river once.
>
> —Cratylus

Killarney, Clapham

Again lies inside the statue the rough lump
the river skims up to. But not for you, not through,
not now, when you snap it up, gecko-
frog-hummingbird 'apprehension', tell it
this is where it's at, illustrate with familiar quotations.
A weedstreaked sphagnum-pitted stone subverts
the formal images it underpins. Twined force
unsprings, uncoils, moles nudge up the ranks
to the tip-tapping up top, where busybody
rivers, grasses, hands caress
waves, intervals between waves not wondering
whether if it can't be done at once
it's not worth doing. So the stone's looked at
in jumble-sales of the head, blind corpse face,
stumbling-block for passing horses, dragonfly larva planet, out
windows into silver running cursive horsemanes on black matt
greening at the silent edges where one stream
undercuts another to the latticed pools.
On the common a big black dog flickering through silver birches
in the snow loses the guild of heralds' bearings
when the water opens out in bloom
ducks in bee-masks make hummingbirds, dance in obscure
    Balinese.

The Scattering Layer

Rain walks all night across the greenhouse roof
on awkward spike-footed stilts, and in the yard, where weeds
and furtive clothespegs interweave, it smears
bluegreen on appleblue leafmould frottage, snaps open
galls where grubs gleam and wrinkle, silverfoil
uncurling waterfalls among the twigs, and cats stare up at
    the stickman.
The stock-car races slide across the compass,
lurch with a crunch and glass breaking up against the end of
    the street,
burglars are picked out in light on the doorsteps, even primroses
glow, and the wingcases of dazed beetles. There are chalk
    diagrams but what goes on
up beyond the Van Allen belt, the scattering layer,
we're not sure: pick up glittering striations, unreadable
    patterns of dots
in the strepitant blueblack undersea rivers, krill or seedspill
raining on us, down here where we swirl in our own light.

The Brazen Head

> The Arabs conducted us to a Labyrinth, where the Ancients bury'd Birds.
>
> —J.F. Gemelli Careri

> I placed a jar in Tennessee...
> It did not give of bird or bush,
> Like nothing else in Tennessee.
>
> —Wallace Stevens

I made a jar past the ten thousand things
bit by bit, day by day, when I came in from the rain,
and it's become by now so particular, the rag-tag
of jars trailing and bobbing after
or popping from encystments in its skin
have dropped like sea-urchin spines
working through, in a consensus
of recalled sunshowers, melted down.
So I can say this,
it is two-handled, of unglazed unpatterned
orangeish earthenware, of a
Dodecanesian design, curve of a caracal's,
a fennec's ears; perhaps fifteen 'inches' tall—
a fingernail in the mind   where it spun up
over the footlight horizon, into the toy
cardboard theatre, head- or crystal ball-sized,
with its odd consistencies of scale, and the way
you bang it with your knuckles and it settles like cats, like snow.

The trouble with these theatres is the script.
The jar rests on a plain pine table
on the whitewashed set that looks with each addition
more like the dining-room at Thoor Ballylee.
The jar's the masking of an inner shape you learn
to take on trust, thinking
'it's neither here nor there', not trying to infer
the 'other side'—but I could slide through
like a grass-snake through a birdcage—

From the webwork world Traherne lost in a pond
fishing from my cardboard box
through frictionless walls of rooms and jars, at night,
its proper world, 'of facts not of things', where nothing
may be and anything may not, the jar purrs.
Our radiotelescopes
will reach out beyond the big bang, and what
it will sound like is one question, and another
what the silence before it will sound like the silence after.

In Transit: A Sonnet Square

for Roseanne

Sydney—Athens—Sydney, November 1979–March 1980

1. Duende in Darlinghurst

If out of our quarrels with ourselves we make poetry, what
do we make of our quarrels with Canberra? Suddenly
someone has gone and invented a new emotion
just as we were coming to terms with Weltschmertz.
Let them in and look what happens.
All the same, the streets are ajitter with larrikins
and outside the boarded-up brothel a tart and her hoon—
    but a cat
from a different poem cuts out, folds itself in
in a lump at the bedfoot; in this universe
cats are sinisterly dextrous; in antiworlds
at the bottom of the class. Feng-shuei, lion and lamb,
    their sadness
of a tightrope walker over shadows. Do we all fall
now like shooting-gallery ducks? There's a kind of snowdrop
that grows, but never flowers, in the lowest circle.

2. Biography

About love and hate and boredom they were equally
barracudas, took an arm or leg quick as winking,
their totem Monkey Aware-of-Vacuity.
Empedocles added to the four elements
Love and Strife to set them spinning, Aeschylus
invented tragedy by adding the second actor.
Back past the sold houses in the lost domains
down in the midden-humus
glows the rotting trelliswork of 'family',
odd slug-coloured tubers wince at the touch
with feigned unanthropomorphic shyness,
naked pink tendrils explore holes. It is all
tentative, and these days the Island supports
a 'Jungian sandlot therapist'.

3. Hecate County

'This faux pas may be on the nose' (SMH crossword)
and while amyl nitrite does give the nostrils a bloom
and the head a rush of fake Pythagorean
claritas—imaginary number, gaily unfecund—the urethritis
goes away of its own accord. Being more at home
always in the abstract, and counting the streaks of the tulip
all too like afterwards asking whether
It Was Good For You Too Darling, remember Edmund Wilson
was cured by silver nitrate, knowing the risks, in
no time. Well, you have ridden away on your bicycle,
Adrian Leverkühn's doctors kept falling down dead
like something out of Straw Peter, the undergoing
of the eveninglands though refuses to focus,
the shimmering spokes setting far in the northwest.

4. The Rout of San Romano; or, Arsenal 3 Manchester United 2

Three goals in the last minutes, when tens of thousands
were already on their way home!—Niccolo da Torentino,
arching truncheoned in the foregound, washed in yellow
green mauve skyblue green yellow, has yet to notice—
there where the shadowline subtends the wave
of breaking colour—the two knights outside the battle
companionably riding up the hill out the back of the canvas
not giving a stuff who wins. And Cattignola only arrives
in the Uffizi; why hang around
so scattered a pictorial space?—the eventual winner
was anyway winning already. The pig-snouted trumpeters,
angelic pigeon-chested page, the 'web of men', foreshortened
in a third of the triptych, are in 'London', in nothing:
turn off the set. And they broke up and scattered across nothing.

5. The Modern Primitive

for Theofilos Hadjimikhail

> Only real loaves of bread fall down. Painted ones stay where you put them.
>
> —Theofilos

He ground his own pigment from brightly coloured stones.
The neighbours stoned him when they found him out
grinding down sea and sky for blues and revealing
a glassy shore-sea full of brightly coloured stones
a thousand fathoms within reach, and only the grey-
olive midworld under a glass sky's
tiny brightly coloured stones' wheeling
glitter a thousand chilly fathoms up. He stood there
stockstill and gave back what he'd stolen:
the glass burst into paint.
The neighbours stoned him and the rocks
hit him exploding steeped in colour:
he ground himself down
and painted all the neighbours' portrait in bright stone.

6. The Café of Situations

for Grace Edwards

In this café they have solved the problem of names.
Orders go to the bar: 'Coffee for Calendar,
two cognacs for Backgammon Board and Football Poster.'
You are where you are. They know names must be revealed
most cautiously and that numbers only serve numbers.
In the café of situations they have found the golden mean:
sit there often enough and you'll win a table and name,
Clock, say, or Air Vent, which feeds not on you but you,
drop in occasionally and you're still gifted
while you're here with just that identity-in-place
you've been so long in quest of. Wherever I go
I wear the café walls around me, and the shuffling step
of the invisible waiters brings subtly misconstrued orders
to Broke or Loving or Drunk or wherever I happen to be.

7. Games and Pastimes I: Chess

Sui-mate: Black moves first and forces White to checkmate him.

Maybe things will improve when Borges becomes the first
to gain a posthumous Nobel. Meanwhile the fifth-floor window
gapes on Luzhin's board; oddly it's no temptation.
Situation: ten days to go in Athens and I can do
one of two things: (a) pay the hotel bill, (b) eat.
In the chessworld web of interconsequence, shall I blame
    Black Holes,
go back in time and shoot my great-great-grandfather?
Both are free like sonnets. For the best effect
you don't strip yourself of all your defences; rather deploy them
as vast as futile, done up with funny faces,
tripping over each other's shoelaces. Spend years learning
what no one wants, then so arrange things
then you can't even do it. Let the sleek-haired Spartans
win Thermopylae. Who needs the epitaph?

8. Games and Pastimes II: Crossword

—Hearing, as I do the crossword, 'You like Turkish coffee?'—
Turkish? in Athens? Outside the donkeyboys
play Ayatollahs. A crimson knot of panzers at the counter
are bawling 'Shrimp! Shrimp!'—I think we're defeated,
and it's as cold as London. The Caryatids' blank niches
wait for amalgam: Seferis' dream—'Yeah man
your little ol' Parthenon'd make a great ad for toothpaste'—
naturalism and a big gold grin. The last clue
looks like a giggle and slides off. In the local paper
'Infant bites snake: a female Herakles?';
an easy one that though, uncryptic, the story begins
'In a suburb of Melbourne, Australia.' O to think
'this isn't "my" Greece'; it never was. With years to run
the phony lease has been scrapped and the demolishers come.

9. Games and Pastimes III: Jigsaw

Everyone in the village sues everyone else over land rights.
This is the literal Arcadia. My book on cryptanalysis
dissolves unnoticed; there's no shower curtain
to the only shower in town. But where else to write
a critical study of SF? My enormous friend
the Christopher Brennan expert, trying to grow
eyes in the back of his head, shatters the plate-glass door.
I talk for three hours about *Sir Gawain and the Green Knight*
till too drunk for pain I smash my jaw on a milepost.
'Jeeze it's great the way you keep it up'; somehow my
    nerve-ends nod
and also the locals think we're CIA. They're throwing the
    blacks in the harbour
and there aren't enough blacks to go around. And while we fall
my other friend works at the Jackson Pollock jigsaw
for the twenty-second year, remarking: 'I'm a slow tourist.'

10. The Plato's Cave Hotel

i.m. Mimis Leoussis

Now his old mansion houses a double ghost.
I've carried the first like a furled handkerchief
twenty years now, since the child's day
they wouldn't let me see him, only the twin shadow
swinging pendulum with the gold-crystal chandelier that's gone
now his house is the hotel where all night I wake, wait, sweat.
I met the second on the hill, in the olive-groves:
Paris-Edwardian fashion catalogues, bills of lading
for timber and sponges and marble; envelopes with his name
in mauve and sepia copperplate; as though in the midday hush
a landau had clip-clopped by and frightened the crickets.
He was whisper-thin and stained as those envelopes, wore
a carnation buttonhole he could no longer afford, and spoke
in copperplate of his ships, the mists of Oxford, the waltzing
    beauties.

11. Of Time and Typing

I sit here writing you letters that always cross
and thinking about time and typing.
Those 'effortless' lyrical tropes, how drearily long they gestated,
'beauty, that unicorn'—fourteen years younger,
proud of how much I knew, how hard I revised.
The terms of the problem have changed: how to answer your last
when your next is on its way without warping both
how to fit the machine with seismograph paper
so as to write the honest poem that's mainly white space
to denote all the hours of just smoking and staring at
    crosswords,
reading and trying not to
auguries in what's not in your letter, drinking
and hopelessly masturbating, knowing the room smells,
the cleaning lady is at the door, the toilet will never flush.

12. Drinking Sappho Brand Ouzo

after Vassilis Vassilikos

Crackup, last day of Carnival, first of Lent,
an ouzo-sodden moony pall hangs over the city
where we swim, soft wet flies, mad and silent
and American sailors on leave, their faces covered
with moist red apertures, buy Greek pornography.
'I only come to observe the audience.'
Cheap ouzo, Sappho brand, the dawn
*b*rododaktulos, in the Lesbian dialect. The normal
awaking hangover this time is milky white not blue,
has the half-twist of sexual origami. Try being stoic
in the Stoa five minutes' walk off—crackup—the sherds
carry dialectal variants of your name, and a gypsy
follows everywhere singing: 'I shook down
the flowers from the blossoming almond-tree.'

13. For the Cretan Maker

> i.m. Nikos Xylouris

> Then he died ... so I made him a song
>
> —General Makriyannis, *Memoirs*

As always, lose a friend and gain an emblem.
So Xylouris is gone too. Unmet, unknown. Oh, hell, hell,
write more poems, half-Berryman would-be Cretan,
sing his lament in the shower? High in the White Mountains
they're listening for the black horseman with the clanging chains
dragging the Heroes; no one is crying, no one.
Cancer of the stomach, nine months. I don't know what's born—
for me—if a billion dead Chinese jumped—
they propped his knife and his lyre against the stone
and named a street after him. And for my mother.
Last night at dinner three shepherds sang his songs
and I did the sort of thing one seems to have done
with the idea of putting it into some tawdry poem—bile,
black bile—I hid my tears behind the TLS.

14. On Aggression: Group Self-Portrait as Greylag Goslings

for LD, JF, GR, JT and MJ

    And home at last between drafts. Back in Athens
air like unwashed dogs, the temples pitted grey, friends passing
leaving me phials of curious pills. Old favourite pin-up
Emperor Julian Apostate, bless
                        these spiralling austerities
as calculated as the filioque. Then flattening air, a flight
more of a waddle, a sling-stretch of the mind
to silicon-chip blackjack and my friends again
in the ruined beer-garden. They've stolen another sky.
    The goslings fight, as do adults, using their wings,
    but as these are no more than tiny stumps, their blows
    fall short, for they aim them as if their wings
    were in the right proportion
                        to the size of their bodies
thus Konrad Lorenz. (It's not the heat
but the humidity. Make love not imprintings.)

Room 23

Love thrives on absence and abhors clear sight—
perhaps. Yet in the fading of late night
each solitary evening, in this room
which piles of books and soap and socks make home
of sorts, pathetically, I know I feel
absences which define this love as real.
Sweet love, to make love isn't all of love
although I ache for it. Even above
delicious privacies, I've understood
even to quarrel with you would be good.
Proust, I suppose, once and for all defined
the intermittencies of heart of mind
whereby the gone becomes the never wanted:
but these Athenian solitudes are haunted
with images of you. At three o'clock
I wake each morning staring at the lock
as though the turning of a key might bring
you suddenly into the room; some spring,
as in a schlocky song, green and make right
the vacant winter's day, the interminable night.

For the Birds: The Life of Paolo Uccello

Uccello once fancied he was turning into cheese,
still, lived 'to a disgruntled eighty-three',
according to the censorious Vasari.
He was the fanatical type, like Spinoza.
He loved pictures of animals and birds,
being unable to afford the creatures themselves
or, like Leonardo, to buy and free them.
When his friend Donatello made fun of him
he stopped painting, saw no one, spent his last years
'solitary, eccentric, melancholy and poor',
working on intricate technical problems.
His wife said he'd refuse to come to bed,
saying 'Oh, what a lovely thing is this perspective!'
He seems to me to have been a happy man.

In the Refectory of the Ognissanti

In the refectory of the Ognissanti
at four in the echoing afternoon
lunch has been left in front of the Last Supper:
three almost empty mineral-water bottles,
breadcrumbs, plastic cups on the trestle table
that seems set up to echo Ghirlandaio's.
You could pass a drink to Judas.
Birds fly out of trompe l'oeil into yesterday's loggia
where Peter's half-raised knife cuts sandwiches.
It's like the recurring 'j'
you change into 'i' when you're editing German,
like the way there's no way
to see the Gattamelata except on TV.
One experience always deflects another,
a billiards of aborted possibilities,
and what you see you've brought with you like a picnic.
You walked into the shaft of light
in the painted background where all the lines met
and it rained uniquely and all day on the poplars,
the burnt-umber castles, the straciatella ice-cream.
The roadside was littered with porcupine quills
like tramps' signs or Ogham. You're a poet,
she said before going, well, here's a quill.
In the refectory of the Ognissanti
you hear in a corner the familiar scuttle
of a theory of aesthetics going to ground.

The fox in the vineyard, the roebuck in the mist
were bright singularities without a syntax,
the distant hills just beyond the window
a russet and green infolding, dimensionless and precise,
and over Pienza a faded rainbow
embodies the idea of destination,
but there's a wall behind the birds.
Now the green grapes are gone, and the speed of fresco
pulls haloes oblate, moons two days off full,
and among more stars than you thought possible
something untimely howling in the woods
that bristle down to the river's edge suggests
alternative skylines best left unpainted. Later,
there's less of the lunch left, though you're still alone.
You thought you'd flattened Ghirlandaio:
you thought a pale blue beehive mattered more.
You try to make your provenance impeccable.
The ancient codices speak of a white tower
floating in silver clouds on the horizon,
a tapestry of insinuating hills. There are directions
for painting blue-green lizards among the blackberries,
an orange three-legged dog breaststroking through long grass,
directions for editing and reattribution.
In the refectory of the Ognissanti
you taste the thin flavour of actuality
you carry around like an abridged Vasari.
Rainwater sinks in and hollows behind your eyes
a workshop where the restorers wash off varnish
and critics scoff at the flat vivid wall
you walk back into, licking melted ice-cream.

Offering up your void, you invent perspective,
the birds fly out of the wall,
perch on the turrets of the unattainable tower
and peck outrageous signatures
on dissolving frescoes you authenticate.
The landscape folds neatly into your head
which you carry carefully as rare majolica
out into the rain that sweeps the Arno,
making sure that nothing rattles.
And very carefully, not stepping on the lines,
you tiptoe like Uccello
in a fevered abstraction of vanishing points,
green slate of the river washed in gunmetal grey,
having your cake and eating it,
from the refectory of the Ognissanti.

His Wife is a Well-Known Criminologiste

Rome from certain angles
is appropriately like a bust of Sigmund Freud
trepanned and bored to expose the limbic system.
The best hotels are in the hypothalamus
where Pasolini got his.
In Trieste, on the other hand, there's no sign of Joyce
and Yugoslavs leave their old shoes
in Tibetan-style cairns outside *calzature* windows.
This is in heatwaves. The best thing to do
is get lost the long way through the Vatican museums
looking for *The School of Athens*, where if not Plato
certainly Aristotle will have an up-to-date timetable.
A dog-eared *Civilisation and its Discontents*
lies open at the dirty bits.

Poise

> But so far there has been no mass influx of tickers and twitchers, although we were joined by one enthusiast from Kent.
>
> —'A Country Diary', *Guardian*, 29 June 1988

Solitude *à deux*: a language consisting largely
of interpolations into the unsaid,
Parthian shots frozen in Zeno's time,
a clock that doesn't tick,
the dog that did nothing in the night-time.
Poise, I admit, eludes me,
like a badly translated handbook of Portuguese etiquette,
a giraffe with rickets,
a reading-lamp pitched awkwardly
to shine not upon the sheet of anxious paper
but into the corner of the writing-desk
where, in a mess of sodden Kleenex,
a woodlouse wriggles on its back
in complicated and unnecessary grief.

The Battle of Trasimene

Of course it was their armour dragged them down.
The Carthaginian wall of eightfold hides
ground bleak as gravity to the lake, and so
the legions sank like lumps of bronze; besides,
there was no other place for them to go.
Look down on a clear day and it replays.
They sway like seaweed; in a blue-green haze
they backpedal and splash a while and drown.
The fat and hopeless couple in the bar,
the spidery girl in the flyblown dress,
the man who screams and curses at the bus,
the elegant scholar patched up with copper wire,
the man who pays the boy to play the clown
of course it was their armour dragged them down.

Hengist and Horsa

The mercenaries refuse to be paid off.
They lounge in corners like sacks of potatoes,
belching, eating the cat. Your best gifts are fraudulent,
they say, in goose-stepping gutturals
of their own, you can tell, *faux-naïf* invention.
You read trains as implying frontiers,
like clocks and clockmakers.
In the random library,
among the grimoires, timetables and cookbooks,
you hit upon the *Lives of Sts Cyril and Methodius*,
wait for the shadow at the door, and study
how to balance finally the exquisite insult
and a receptiveness instinct with the humility
of a bowl of milk rapturously receiving cornflakes.

Sweet Dreams

Failure to master the polite use of *Lei*
is perhaps the least of my worries, but haunts my sleep
in whinny-tangles of misunderstanding.
'Sedentary, arrogant and solipsistic,'
judges the water-diviner, bustling back into the wood.
Wine weaves a shroud of unspecific ghosts,
fissile as amoebas but with insect feet.
Something tall and phallic lurches toward the bed.
Absences solidify like terra-cotta
pangolin-shaped urns with clacking scales.
The night's full of spikes;
on them
hangs a vast flabby thing with the face of a frog.
Tomorrow I shall study the Cultural Revolution.

Biennale, After Magritte

Consciousness regarded as an empty window
interrupted by the distant flight of a bird
or a cloud in tempera on eggshell-blue gesso
offers a crossroads of possibilities
you can always call internalised,
at least if you're writing a poem.
And if you're not
you can draw on garbled memories of King Kong and Godzilla,
the hunter-observer snug in his hide
in the fork of the tree by the swamp
while low in the corner of the flickering screen
the horrible thing rises and reaches out,
all the more terrifying
for being, really, so shoddily put together.

Biennale: The Romanian Pavilion

In the Romanian pavilion the terror
is both dead and charming, and a young woman sits
knitting at the door, acting log-ignorant
of being both hackneyed and emblematic,
a garbled half-educated quote.
George Meredith, too, comes to mind: rank on rank,
the army of unalterable law—
but not the stars. But wicker coffins. But—
are the allusions deliberate? Have they nothing better
to do in Romania?
Sprung at last, I sit and sip beer
in wet flat sunlight, and watch seven cats
out of the corner of my eye making a pattern
beautiful, unpremeditated, not to do with words.

Gorey at the Biennale

The vaporetto founders in green slush,
wickerwork masks are hanging in the trees
aslant, with half-glimpsed smiles. A vague unease
seems to be centred on a certain bush.
Those little birds seem not quite right for birds,
these beetles have an odd seductive air.
Who ever heard of willow trees with hair?
Words keep suggesting other unwanted words.
It's not that it's not pretty in the park,
not that you feel there's anything afoot,
but when you hear the little steamer's toot
you hurry to get out before it's dark.
Of course the gate is locked; of course you knew
the star attraction of the show was you.

Central American Football

Today I saw my first tophet and my first chac-mool.
Fat Venice blazed and the canals steamed upward,
air between palaces
latticed all of a sudden with the skeletons of extinct fish.
The Phoenicians; Mexico Before Columbus;
7000 lira a pop; why not?
    Why not burn babies? The heatwave drags us off
to the La Brea tarpits and the Danish bogs.
The sand gapes and swallows.
The patient chac-mool grins in the next gallery
in the attitude of Alcibiades at the feast—
what a time to be reading Malcolm Lowry—
stone scroll unfolded deftly
waiting for the plop of the newborn screaming heart

Tabula Rasa

The hoopla! clang and return of the typewriter carriage
invests each line with a finally spurious authority.
The same is true of the genre of 'nature poems'.
Birdlife regarded as historically portentous
or the cypresses as spelling out something in Umbrian
have all the easy felicity of soap.
The marquetry of incandescent cumulus over the hilltops
is an exercise in mere rococo; while in the village,
pointlessly, the Christian Democrats are dancing.
Rain sweeps in from Lago Trasimene
in this season of mauve flowers after the season of yellow.
I would hold, in point of making a statement,
against the nightingale's obstinate aria
the lit and utter silence of fireflies.

Getting to Know the General

Splotches of green fingerpaint on Tuscan brown,
a background iridescent with fine detail
in which each dewdrop stares back thoughtfully
from its idealised position on the leaf
till two small girls wipe it all out in glee.
An exercise in metrics takes you back
to portraits of heroes in the whitewashed schoolroom
and a language you couldn't yet quite understand.
Getting to know the general is an exercise
in stretching characters beyond their limits
obliquely to edge past time that lies in wait
in the alley of cypresses that aren't the past
of anyone but you, and seem to know it.
He wasn't on the posters, and his handwriting
took seventeen months just to decipher.
Time carries bowls of glue and wicked fish-hooks
laid out in the semblance of an alphabet,
a script like wind-swirls in sand or the pattern of frogs
criss-crossing the pond under the smudge of algae
when a football in the rain drenches them in fear.
Time looks like a big-character poster
merging into a gnarled sandstone wall
and warning of wicker men and man-traps
past the next turning, just over the hill,
the only place the road leads to.
Or in the dim waiting-room they punch tickets,
rip open suitcases full of old papers,
tell fortunes with balls of string.

By the roadside there are rocks with eyes
and lizards' tails flicking in the long grass
and a tattered page out of Ouspensky.
The brigands with their silver guns pour through the passes,
melons and lemons ripen in the sun,
the fishing boats come back empty day after day.
The general has a word with you
in a little-known northern dialect. The next uncut page
trembles in a fever of pathetic fallacy
and opens impossibly upon a folksong
about mermaids and riders in rose-green cloaks.
In the past the fig trees wear the walls down,
the towns unbuild themselves to bedrock,
usurers haggle in the village square.
On the curving road to the abbey you realise
your map is of another country, and the famous frescoes
are tipped-in plates in primary colours
in a book too heavy to take with you on the journey.
In the waiting-room they serve the ghost of coffee,
your passport and ticket are lost in a different story
and the singers lose the thread and start again.
Brilliantly coloured birds buck the wind
and across the green valley sheep spell out
stinging reviews of *The Structure of Complex Words*.
Making no sense, the visa bursts into flower,
then crawls off the page on scores of furry legs.

In the past the dust-motes in the corners of your eyes
spread out flat into a stained chart of islands,
a plumb-line, a leather pouch, a well.
The sun broods around the windows,
in the slate silence a rattle of beads,
the click of a flick-knife or a leaf falling
into the well of noon disturb the surface,
then sink into a matting of fragmentary texts.

Your time runs out halfway through learning
Old Church Slavonic, a cure for the common cold
and the tactics of bribery. Birdsong hurts.
In the past they keep rewriting the rulebook.
The general's hunched up in shadow at a desk
behind strings of onions and barrels of salt cod,
spelling out simple words. He thanks you politely
for your beautiful gifts, and paints you
a foursquare house in beechwoods, labelled 'house',
and a knife called 'money'. Then he goes to sleep.

They keep bits of the past in a box in Leningrad
in a room washed with green light
where engineers' mandibles click in chorus
and a thin hum seeps out from a bubble of black glass.
There are no cats in this poem, but if there were
they'd be the scrawny cats of nostalgia
living on breadcrumbs filtered through the screen of trees.
You try reading Auden. Why does he write in Pushtu?
You cut out a string of little dancing men
and try to cheat the customs officers
with bunches of purple grapes, and tattered chapbooks
full of lies about Alexander the Great.
The cypresses float on the horizon
at midnight above the ruined theatre
where piles of obsolete silver coins gleam in the moonlight.
You try to find the right page in the phrasebook
but all you get is 'Booking a Hotel'.
You fish up something from the well,
fish-belly white, with scarlet maggots,
gift-wrap it, learn another language,
you try giving the archivists baksheesh.

As you patch up a broken syllable
you see that while you've been at work
the crones have jumped the queue. In the waiting-room
a trapdoor slides open, canvas flaps, a gust of wind
slaps open a sackful of dust. In the next room
the general is picking jonquils. The doors are all nailed shut.

Writing in the Manner of ...

Writing in the manner of, say, Auden is easy
when you're nervous enough, and right now I'm very nervous
but not, as you see, writing in the manner of Auden,
in itself no small achievement,
nor even in that of Berryman,
rather in a manner enacting, by design or not,
a strange brew of melancholy and agitation
and a naive-dualistic awareness
of myself aware of the whole farrago
and of not being allowed to represent it
either in tensile and ambiguous steel
or in wit's sheen and belly
but in a long limp single sentence
leaving behind it, out of the poem, leftovers, a trail of crumbs.

Grief

for Roseanne

Grief breaks the heart and yet the grief comes next.
Some lemon morning in a wash of rain
a brand-new horror comes to call again
and write a footnote to expunge the text.

The gall slips down and hardly hurts at all;
your scholarly rescensions of the past
prove to your satisfaction that at last
time counterloops and paradoxes pall.

Your paintings have been swapped for cheap engravings,
all trace of colour has been washed away,
it's 3 a.m. although you know it's day,
the bank's engrossed your past and future savings.

    Love is the subject and love's loss the text.
    Grief breaks the heart and yet the grief comes next.

Notes by Martin Johnston on 'To the Innate Island'

Perhaps those who are annoyed by provisos, detainments and postscripts could be persuaded to take probity on faith and disregard the notes.

—Marianne Moore

It is impertinent to suggest that the reader ought to possess already any odd bit of information ...

—William Empson

That Poésie should be as perviall as Oratorie, and plainness her special ornament, were the plaine way to barbarisme ... Obscuritie in affectation of words and in digested concepts, is pedenticall and childish; but where it shroudeth it self in the hart of his subject, uttered with fitness of figure, and expressive Epethites; with that darkness will I still labour to be shadowed.

—George Chapman

1. The Shadow Screen

Setting: 'the literal Arcadia'; the fishing village of Paralion Astros ('Star-on-Sea'), situated on what used to be an island but has gradually been silted-up into a peninsula. The nearby convent of Loukou, on the site of the villa of Herod Atticus, is incongruously adorned with Herod's collection of statues of the Olympian gods. After the War of Independence it became modern Greece's first museum.

For the village, the sea and the cat, see 'Microclimatology'.

2. Finding Islands

Setting: the 'hanging' monasteries of Meteora in Thessaly; and Yannina, capital of Epirus. Much of the background is conveniently accessible in English in Patrick Leigh Fermor's *Roumeli*, chapters 1, 2 and 5. Cf. also James Merrill's poem 'Yannina'.

Line 2: from a song by Yannis Markopoulos and Yannis Maris.

Lines 1–3: cosmogony courtesy of Laplace more than Hesiod.

Lines 10–11: cf. Markopoulos/Maris, 'The Mad Monk', and George Seferis's essay on the rock-hewn monasteries of Cappadocia in *Dhokimes*, vol. 2 (only in Greek).

Line 12ff: The island—unnamed—in Lake Pamvotis ('All-feeder'), Yannina; of which Lambros Malamas observes, in *A Tourist Guide of Epiros*, that 'it forms a semicircle long and narrow like half a moon. It looks like a floating cradle on the water of the lake ... The history of the Island is mystical, but contains much instructive information.'

Line 13: Kyria Frossyni and her sixteen attendant ladies, drowned in the lake in 1801, for erotico-political reasons, by the then tyrant of Epirus, Byron's good mate Ali Pasha. Ballads about this are still sung (and postcards sold).

Lines 15–20: Meteora. The monasteries look so inaccessible that the locals believe (or used to) that their founders arrived on eagles.
 Theofanis: major representative of the Cretan school of post-Byzantine ikon painting whose best-known product is Domenikos Theotokopoulos (El Greco). Iconographical motifs and folksongs alike spread northward from Crete via wandering painters.

Line 25: Aristotle and his followers; Dionysus of Syracuse, whom Plato vainly hoped to turn into a Philosopher-King.

Line 28ff: more wanderers: The Sarakatsan and Vlach nomads of the north and the wandering thieves of Kravara in Aetolia, some of whom did in fact find their way to Manchuria and Siberia. The Vlachs have their own language, the Sarakatsan their own dialect, the Kravarites a thieves' argot. The Koutsovlachs of Metsovo speak a form of camp-Latin.

Lines 35–36: 'they move...', from Malamas, on the eels of Pamvotis; 'only antinomian...', from Saul Bellow, *Humboldt's Gift*: here, *inter alia*, a glancing reference to Delmore Schwartz and John Berryman.

3. The Ikonostasis

Same settings as 2. Specifically, the monastery of St Panteleimon on the island in Pamvotis, where Ali Pasha was himself assassinated in 1882 by agents of the Sultan; and which now houses an Ali Pasha museum, featuring a lifesize doll in the clothes of Ali's mistress Kyria Vassiliki.

Lines 13–17: the convent of Roussianou at Meteora; cf. *Roumeli*, chapter 2.

4. Cross in the Water

Paralion Astros, modulating to Lake Pamvotis. As part of Epiphany celebrations in Greece, the local priest or bishop throws a cross into the sea (if available; otherwise whatever body of water there is) and youths dive in to retrieve it.

Line 7: Chinese dragons, unlike western ones, are, at least in their intentions, usually benign; though sea-dragons can inadvertently cause typhoons on rising to the surface. For more on these, on the All-Compassionate Boddhisattva Kuan-yin, on 'airy bureaucrats' etc., see Wu Ch'eng-en, *Monkey*. Cf. also Jorge Luis Borges, *The Book of Imaginary Beings*, Bernard Heuvelmans, *Sea-Serpents*, and Richard Carrington, *Mermaids and Mastodons*.

Line 9: gorgon: in post-classical Greece, not one of the petrifying sisterhood of mythology but the alarming Greek mermaid, whose habit it is to demand of passing ships whether Alexander the Great still lives. In response to any reply other than 'He lives and reigns', she sinks the ship. Needless to say, Greek seamen tend to be familiar with the correct formula. For an enfeebled western version of this legend, see James Elroy Flecker's poem 'Santorin'.

Line 10: priests on boats bring terrible luck.

Line 16: cf. the Theravada Buddhist classic *Milinda-Panha (The Questions of King Milinda),* which recounts the conversion by the monk Nagasena of the Graeco-Bactrian ruler Menandros (Milinda); it also adumbrates the doctrine of Boddhisattvas. See (e.g.) Christmas Humphreys, *Buddhism*; Joseph W. Campbell, *The Masks of God,* Vol. 2: *Oriental Mythology.*

Lines 10, 20, 21: Iskander, Aristu, Aflatun are the Arabic versions of Alexander, Aristotle and Plato respectively. One ought to mention here the medieval Arabic legend about Aristotle and Plato sailing round the world and, on their return, meeting themselves setting off; or—should one say?—setting off round the world despite seeing their aged and ragged selves returning. There's a Flecker version of this too: 'The Ballad of Iskander'.

Line 21ff: transition from Paralion Astros to Pamvotis, via an imaginary performance of *Karaghiozis*, the Greek shadow-pupper theatre (on which see Sotiris Spatharis, *Behind the White Screen*).

Line 31ff: transition/allusion to 'certaine Players at Exeter, acting upon the stage the tragical storie of Dr. Faustus the Conjurer', who suddenly perceived that 'there was one devell too many amongst them; and so after a little pause desired the people to pardon them, they could go no further with this matter; the people also understanding the thing as it was, every man hastened to be first out of dores'. (Quoted in E.K. Chambers, *The Elizabethan Stage;* there are versions in John Aubrey, and in the Puritan William Prynne's *Histrio-Mastix*.)

Lines 31–40, simultaneously: return to Kyria Frossyni.

5. The Monemvasia Causeway

This section is in part a tribute to the poet Yannis Ritsos, whose birthplace Monemvasia (or Malmsey—as in Clarence, or vice versa) is. Monemvasia is a Byzantine town, massively fortified, on a great rock linked by a causeway to the mainland of the south-east Peloponnese. Here it's conflated with the Byzantine ghost town of Mystra, near Sparta ('the Greek Pompeii'—Kazantzakis) which, for a few years after the fall of Constantinople, *was* the Byzantine Empire. Here the last of the Palaeologus dynasty squabbled over a kingdom consisting of a hill, while Gemistus Plethon elaborated the last of the pagan-syncretistic philosophies. Mystra was burned by the Albanians in 1740, but much remains. It broods, as well it might.

Line 4: in Greece the telling of fairy- or folk-tales is conventionally likened to the unwinding of a spool of red thread.

6. Friezes

Setting: various genuine and/or Malraux-esque museums and art galleries; and Mount Pelion, Thessaly, which is associated with Achilles, Chiron and Jason and with the Titans. Cf. 'Microclimatology'.

Line 6: Prometheus, of course.

7. From the Folk-Song Archives

Crete, Thessaly, Macedonia, Epirus. For the underlying metaphor here and in section 10, 'Psychopannychy', see what little literature there is on the concept of 'mental maps'; also Albert B. Lord. *The Singer of Tales.*

Lines 1–2: a common motif in ikons, e.g. in St Varlaam, Meteora.

Lines 7–11: cf. section 2, lines 15–20.

Line 16: cf. section 4, line 21ff. And, again, *Behind the White Screen.*

Line 19: Dante's Odysseus (*Inferno* XXVI), not Homer's or Joyce's.

Line 21: the satyr Marsyas, flayed alive by Apollo after unsuccessfully challenging him to a music contest.

The Greek revolutionary Dionysios Skylosofos was similarly flayed by the Turks at Yannina in 1611; his skin was stuffed with straw and exhibited *pour encourager les autres*. The Incas, on the other hand, made drums of their captives' skins and flutes of their bones: cf. section 12.

Line 22: kastura: see 'Ode for St Cecilia's Day' in A.D. Hope, *New Poems 1965–1969*. Zalongo: in 1803 the Greek stronghold of Souli, on the coast of Epirus, fell by treachery to the Turks. The few women who survived the ensuing massacre sang and danced their way, one by one, off the nearby precipice of Zalongo. (The song survives.)

Line 23: for the bell, see Octave Mirbeau, *The Garden of Tortures.*

8. The Bills

Paralion Astros again: a domestic scene for once.

Line 26: my version of Kepler comes mainly from Arthur Koestler, *The Sleepwalkers* and Marie Boas, *The Scientific Renaissance, 1450–1630*.

Line 28: Robert Frost, 'Design'.

9. A Drink at the Exploding Monastery

Crete in general, and the monastery of Arkadhi, near Chania, in particular. During the abortive 1855 Cretan uprising against the Turks a force of guerrillas, besieged in this monastery, blew it up, killing themselves and a high proportion of their assailants. One or two children are reputed to have survived the explosion; in Chania I met a very old man who claimed to have met one of these; but then 'all Cretans are liars'.

Lines 26–29: cf. the opening chapters of Lyall Watson, *The Romeo Error*.

10. Psychopannychy

'The condition of the sleeping soul between death and the Resurrection.' This section constitutes a more or less direct continuation of section 9.

    Setting: Lake Pamvotis; Meteora; various northern Greek churches and monasteries (e.g. the church in Kastoria whose fresco-painter was struck blind for the blasphemy of having depicted God the Father); a sort of afterlife. And cf. 'Microclimatology'.

11. Water-Garden Snapshots

Paralion Astros and Crete, especially in Minoan sites at Knossos and Phaistos. Leading on to:

12. The Whistlers of Phaistos

Mainly Phaistos itself, with interwoven allusions to South America, notably the Incas and Pablo Neruda. Cf. the relevant sections of J. M. Christoforakis, *Crete: A Complete Travellers' Guide*. The poem as a whole rummages around various versions of—as it happens—

Greece. It is searching, as hindsight reveals, for the Phaistos Disc; finds it; fails, however, to decipher it.

Line 15: Messara stretches between Phaistos and the Libyan Sea.

Lines 29–30: Etymologically, astrolabe = star-taker.

Line 37: according to the ancient Cretans, not only was the cave of Diktys the birthplace of Zeus, but he was reborn there every year; hence, indeed, the belief of more orthodox Greeks that all Cretans were liars. See the sections on theogony in Robert Graves, *The Greek Myths*.

Lines 38, 47, 59: snake-worship in various forms was common to early Greek and pre-Columbian American cultures; and Tiresias got the way he did through seeing snakes mating; while the oracle of Delphi originated through the combat of Apollo and the chthonian Thing, Python. On all this, cf. Campbell, *The Masks of God, passim*.

Lines 52–53: an early attempt to decipher Linear B. Ventris and Chadwick did better.

Lines 56–59: cf. G.K. Chesterton's poem 'Lepanto'.

Line 60: on the Triple Goddess, see Graves, and any number of Minoan rings.

Copyright

Poems and notes by Martin Johnston
copyright © Vivienne Latham 2020

Introduction and selection
copyright © Nadia Wheatley 2020

First published in 2020 by Ligature Pty Limited.
34 Campbell St · Balmain NSW 2041 · Australia
www.ligatu.re · mail@ligatu.re

ISBN 978-1-925883-26-8

All rights reserved. Except as provided by fair dealing or any other exception to copyright, no part of this book may be reproduced or transmitted in any form or by any means without permission in writing from the publisher.

The moral rights of the author are asserted throughout the world without waiver.

ligature*fi*nest

www.ingramcontent.com/pod-product-compliance
Lightning Source LLC
Chambersburg PA
CBHW021436080526
44588CB00009B/552